Slavery in the West

With a special emphasis on the events leading to

The Battle of Rock Creek
El Dorado County California 1848

Between the forces of the Miwok versus the Maidu and Washoe

Also the First and Second Indian Wars of
El Dorado County

The untold story of the slavery of Native Americans in the West

By Guy Nixon
(Red Corn)

In the Spirit of my Grandfather's Grandfather
Claws of the Red Panther Bill Nixon Red Corn of the Middle Rivers Band
of the Great Osage Tribe

Editor and Research Assistant
Ben Atojino-Carrillo

Copyright © 2012 by Guy Nixon (Red Corn).

Library of Congress Control Number:		2011906830
ISBN:	Hardcover	978-1-4628-6526-0
	Softcover	978-1-4628-6525-3
	Ebook	978-1-4628-6527-7

This book was printed in the United States of America.

Rev. date: 08/02/2013

To order additional copies of this book, contact:
Xlibris LLC
1-888-795-4274
www.Xlibris.com
Orders@Xlibris.com
98751

TABLE OF CONTENTS

4

The view of Yamanim from No-Po-Chitta Toma and Hekeke Toma located in the heart of the Southern Maidu lands. The Battle of Rock Creek
(Wokitto-oosew) took place in the bottom of the Canyon to the far right
where Syhylim Sewim meets Rock Creek. Why did the Miwok have a battle with the Maidu and their Washoe allies? Why here? The answers help to
explain much of the history of the West.

The Turtle (K-ocoj) at Hanks Exchange one of   (Om-Blu-Kai) a "Talking Rock" Squaw Hollow
the "Talking Rocks"   El Dorado County.

Introduction

Very few people realize that a large percentage of Native Americans were taken into slavery and that some of their living descendents would not get their freedom in the United States until 1911, with those in Mexico not for another two decades more. Few realize how international Geopolitics affected the lives of even the most remote populations of Native Americans.

The perceptions of many people today, as well as the Americans coming to California in 1849, were that the area seemed a wilderness untouched by the rest of the world. They considered the Native peoples of the area primitive and uneducated, worshiping Pagan gods and doing things that made no logical sense. This perception could not be further from the truth, the technological achievements made by these people are only now beginning to be realized.

These are numerous diaries, journals, reports and stories that have been written about this time and area. While each is a fascinating thread of history there hasn't been a comprehensive analysis of just how these threads were woven together to make the fascinating fabric of history for this area. Single threads need to be placed in the context of the others for a clear picture to develop, in many of our accounts the face value is misleading without the analysis of that writers point of view and objectives.

The Lady of the Lake overlooking Lake

In this work I would like to point out the various factors that affected the Native Americans in the West and particularly in Northern California. I am not attempting to make a complete and detailed history but rather to give the reader a deeper appreciation for this history and the people wrapped up in it.

Slavery before the coming of Columbus.

Slavery as an institution was rather limited on the North American continent prior to the coming of Europeans.

I am defining slavery as a permanent multi generational class of people in servitude for an indefinite period of time.

The largest number of slaves in Pre-Columbian North America was in the Aztec Empire. These people served in agriculture or were used as sacrificial victims for the Aztec priests. The numbers of these sacrificial victims as denoted by the Spanish seemed inflated but recent archeological evidence has confirmed that these numbers were correct. Still while this is the largest number of slaves it was a relatively small percentage of the population at large.

North West Coast cultures were urban, based on industries.

While many tribes did have limited enslavement of individuals, they were usually processed into the tribes society and eventually became full citizens or at the very least their children would be full members of the society. The existence of a permanent group of enslaved people was very limited.

It wasn't that the Native Americans had some higher moral code, when slavery became profitable many tribes who had not practiced slavery began to have slaves and began the business of enslaving other Native Americans. It was simply that most Native American societies were based on hunting and gathering with limited reliance on agriculture. The idea of having slaves made no economic sense as it wouldn't add anything to their economic stability or make their lives any easier.

Even those societies who were based on agriculture and who probably would benefit from having slaves saw limited benefit as it would be very difficult to constrain these slaves from running away and the crop output

Cherokee Home surrounded by their fields of corn, squash and beans.

that could be increased was still going to be largely consumed by the very slaves that produced it.

The only region of North America with a large percentage of the population being a permanent multigenerational subclass serving an indefinite period of servitude was the Pacific Northwest's fishing-based societies.

This totem of President Abraham Lincoln located in Saxmon Alaska is actually a Shame Pole carved by the Tlingit Tribe.

Alaska's slavery is a case in point. The Abraham Lincoln totem located in Saxmon Alaska has been misunderstood for better than a century.

The Abraham Lincoln Totem in Saxmon is actually a Shame Pole made by the Tlingit tribe. It was meant to shame the US Government into paying the Tlingit Tribe for the loss of their property that was taken by the US Government. The property taken though was the Tlingit's SLAVES.

As a matter of record it is estimated that approximately 36% of the Native population of Southeast Alaska were slaves.

This figure is comparable to the Southern United States in the 1860 census where the total percentage of the population South of the Mason Dixon Line in slavery was 32%.

9

Much to the surprise of most people today these Northwest communities were large urban settlements with high population densities and a high degree of specialization. These societies were making and using mechanical equipment including the wheel. This equipment was primarily fishing wheels and hoists and rigging necessary for their ships, nets and whaling equipment. These societies were technologically advanced with a great number of specialized professionals.

The fishing and whaling industry was very profitable and there was always an open and willing market for any extra products they could produce. To increase production all they needed was more labor, with slaves came a higher standard of living and an easier life.

An example of the totem poles dedicated to American President Abraham Lincoln by the former Indian slaves.

Due to the urban environment and the geographical boundaries typical to these areas, slaves would have a great deal of difficulty escaping unnoticed and could easily be run down. With watercraft connecting settlements a slave revolt could be put down quickly as reinforcements could be drawn from other areas very quickly.

While the figures are difficult to get for pre-Columbian times the Klamath tribe at the time of the American Civil War was recorded as having over 70% of their population being slaves. One way of estimating the percentage of slaves is by looking at the totem poles.

Most of the Northwest fishing cultures had totem poles as family records. Shortly after the American Civil War it was noticed that many totem poles had what looked like the face of Abraham Lincoln carved on them, complete with his top hat. When asked about it the people said yes it was Abraham Lincoln since he had freed them. By looking at the percentage of totem poles with Abe on them relative to those without, it was apparent that a large percentage of families had been slaves up until the American Civil War.

This figure was roughly the same for most of these communities with possibly higher rates on some island communities where the physical boundary enabled the masters to control the even higher percentage of slaves.

This system was similar to that of Sparta during the Greek Republic. The slave owners kept their slaves in line by killing any slaves who showed incentive to revolt or escape. The other slaves could be kept in service by inflicting physical punishments that stopped short of disabling their ability to produce. This slave class enabled a working class of professionals to specialize in certain technologies giving the ruling class a very high standard of living sustained by their slaves. This system stretched from Southeast Alaska South to the coast of central California.

As for the rest of North America, slaves existed but usually only for such time as was required to integrate them into the society and develop the trust necessary to allow them to become full citizens. Even if the individual did not become a full citizen their offspring would.

It wasn't that the North American tribes had a particularly higher sense of morality. Even tribes that had never practiced slavery became involved in it to a very high degree once it became profitable. The lack of widespread slavery was simply because it wasn't of any particular economic advantage. Even tribes that were largely agriculturally based would have little real advantage in owning slaves. For one, the increased output would be marginal relative to the increased consumption and the security necessary to confine and control a large percentage of slaves was far more trouble than it was worth.

One thing that should be considered was the situation where slaves might come from. The usual cause of slaves was as a result of combat with another tribe in which some or all of the other tribe was defeated and at the mercy of the victors. The wanton and senseless killing of the other tribe's members would make no sense, but releasing them would only mean that they would reappear to be an enemy in the future. So what options could the winner choose?

Osage Warrior with a traditional War Club

For an example I'll use an historical event from my own tribe. The Osage Tribe owned the present states of Missouri, Arkansas, Oklahoma and Kansas. They were primarily based on agriculture with large established towns fed by cultivated crops of corn, beans and squash along the fertile river bottoms as well as domesticated turkey and rabbits. This diet was augmented by hunting deer, bear and other small game locally, along with bi-annual hunts for buffalo in the Western end of their territory.

Durring the 1820's the Arapahoe and Kiowa Apache began raiding Osage towns in the Western areas, taking people and grain. By 1832 the Osage decided to hold a war counsel to develop a plan for dealing a decisive blow to end these raids. The supplies and organization for an Osage Army were developed, along with an operational plan for catching the raiders in the summer of 1833.

The first event was when an Osage army was found by a large group of Kiowa Apache. The Apache vastly outnumbered the Osage Unit and began an attack. The Osage had a unique bow design, using Osage Orange wood, and backed with sinew, the Osage bow was the most powerful in North America. As a point of fact, in a study done in 2008, the Osage Bow was scientifically compared to the Mongolian Bow, English   long Bow and Horn Laminate Bow; the Osage Bow was by far the most powerful, giving it the longest effective range. The secret was that the Osage Orange used in these bows only grew, in a suitable way for bows, inside the area controlled by the Osage Tribe.

This proved such an advantage that despite repeated attacks by the Kiowa Apache not a single Osage was even touched by a Kiowa arrow. The Kiowa lost so many warriors to the Osage arrows that they finally gave up as they could not afford to lose any more warriors.

The Battle became known as the Cutthroat Gap Massacre and even the Kiowa admitted they had not been able to hurt even one Osage warrior.

Later in the summer of 1833 three Osage armies waited for the Red River to lood to block the retreat of the raiding Arapahoe. When the river flooded the Osage moved in a three pronged pincer movement, which pinned the Arapahoe on the East side of the Red River, leaving them at the mercy of the Osage armies. When the Arapahos tried to break out, the Osage slaughtered them because the Arapahos couldn't shoot their arrows far enough to even touch the Osage. The Arapahoe surrendered and the Osage could have taken the Arapahoe as slaves, but the difficulty in keeping the Arapahoe as farm workers made enslaving them of limited value; however, slaughtering the Arapahoe in this condition held no honor for the Osage.

The Osage decided instead to use their war clubs to break every Arapaho warriors right elbow and then turn them lose to return to the rest of their tribe. This way these Arapaho warriors would consume supplies and be a constant reminder to all the Arapaho of what would happen if they raided the Osage again. It wasn't that the Osage had anything against slavery, it just wasn't the best choice available. I would venture to say that this line of reasoning was probably why slavery was so limited in North America's native populations.

The dramatic toll on Native Americans from slavery is poorly documented and rarely discussed. The history of this institution and it's effects throughout the history of the Westward expansion of Europeans deserves explanation.

Any informed look at the history of the West has to be taken in context with the world events that were occurring at that time. These world events had a dramatic effect on events inside this continent.

Nothing happens in a vacuum, and even the most remote Indian tribes in Western North America were often dramatically affected by events happening on the other side of the world.

It should also be noted that this was the time of Empires. Nations that we have come to know in post-World War II behaved very differently in the earlier two centuries. These nations were the very antithesis of modern international diplomacy.

Every nation was out to get what it could with little (if any) regard for any sort of morality. Even the Catholic church was divided in it's desire for wealth and desire to be true to it's teachings.

The Native Americans were out to get the best deal they could get and the Europeans were out to get the best deal they could get, the only rule was there were no rules.

With this in mind, I would like to give a short summary of the world events by these nations that were affecting North America and how these were interrelated with local events.

The Spanish and Portuguese

After decades of war the Spanish finally defeated the Moslem invasion of Western Europe. They were the first Western European Country to fit our modern standard. Their neighbor Portugal had explored the coast of Africa South to the Cape, then East to India and was reaching for China. Their new colonies in India were bringing tremendous wealth to Portugal. Spain was relieved from war in 1492 by liberating Seville from the Moslems and wanted to get some of the wealth and trade that was happening for Portugal. With Christopher Columbus Spain verified the existence of a land to the West across the Ocean.

The gold taken by the Conquistadores proved that there must be more in the ground of the New World. The Spanish were defeating native American empires and building an enormous empire for themselves. Spain soon claimed the Western side of South America, most of the islands of the Caribbean and the Southern part of North America.

Realizing the potential Portugal was soon in possession of the Eastern part of South America but didn't find any Native American empires full of gold in their areas.

The Spanish began to order the Native Americans to bring them more and more gold but it was evident that the natives were not organized to actually mine the gold. The Spanish soon organized the mining, reaping tremendous amounts of gold and silver; so much so that they were causing the price of gold in Europe to drop (inflation of the currency). Other European countries and citizens couldn't buy as much of any goods or product with their gold or silver, as they had only a few years before.

The financial turmoil caused by all this forced many nations to have to go looking for resources outside their borders as well.

Portugal's colonies in Western Africa, necessary for supplying ships going to and from their colony in Western India offered African slaves, but there was virtually no market for them.

As European diseases began to devastate a larger and larger percentage of the Native American population the demand for labor increased. The answer to their problem was importing African slaves. The African slaves were easy to identify and were immune to many of the European diseases, many to Malaria, in addition they were cheap.

Little do we realize that the West African tribes had practiced slavery long before the coming of the Europeans. Due to the nearly constant state of tribal wars in Western Africa (primarily due to a limited food supply), there was a problem for the winning tribes. What could they do with their defeated enemies? The Portuguese were spreading Christianity and were telling those who would listen that it was wrong to kill the helpless, now there was an answer to this problem. Starting with the Portuguese the victorious African tribes would virtually give their defeated enemies to the Europeans to dispose of them. The Victorious African tribes felt that if it was against the Christian God to kill the helpless, then the followers of that Christian God should know what to do with these defeated enemies. It would be the Europeans problem to feed and take care of them.

The Portuguese began to set up slave markets in Brazil while the Spanish set up markets in Cuba. The Spanish and Portuguese developed operations with facilities along the West African coast to receive slaves brought from the interior by other African tribes. These were processed and then shipped to either Cuba or Brazil. Both the Spanish and Portuguese colonies wanted men to work their mines.

The death rate for miners was incredible. The factors of disease, cave ins, accidents and suffocation were augmented by exposure to toxic gasses and metal vapors. The mines consumed men in tremendous quantities.

The problem faced by both the Spanish and Portuguese was that the West African tribes were selling their defeated enemies lock-stock-and-barrel. They had to take the whole lot including the women and children. The idea of sending women or little children into mines went against Catholicism, the answer was to sell the women and children cheap for farm laborers. This would liquidate the problem. For the new sugar and sorghum plantations on the Caribbean islands it was the start of a new level of prosperity. For the English colonies in North America, it was the establishment of slavery as an institution that had never been prominent in English society before. The moral questions and their political consequences would plague the continent for more than three hundred years.

It was the establishment of this institution as a business that was to plague the Native Americans even longer than the descendants of the African Slaves.

The Source's of Slaves for the New World and some common misconceptions.

It should be pointed out that there are several misconceptions about the sources of slaves and about the institution of slavery.

While the Spanish and Portuguese had found that the native populations could not sustain the necessary numbers of laborers needed for their new colonies and that African slaves were better suited for the labor, there were other factors that came into play.

In the beginning of the 1600's King James II of England began the conquest of Ireland. The Battle of Kinsale produced a large number of Irish prisoners of war which were sold as slaves to Portuguese settlements along the Amazon River.

When the English General Oliver Cromwell landed in Ireland and began the comprehensive defeat of the Irish, the numbers involved skyrocketed. In 1649 in Drogheda Ireland alone Cromwell's army killed an estimated 30,000 Irish.

The Irish Confederation and the War to defeat it from 1641 to 1652 killed an estimated 500,000 Irish. The payment for service in this war to Cromwell's officers and men was supposed to be in the form of Irish lands and valuables.

The war had generated an enormous number of widows and orphans. The forced displacement of Irish populations from large tracts of land generated still more displaced Irish people.

In an effort to generate revenue to pay for the war, Cromwell's Council State in 1656 ordered 2000 Irish Children, between the ages of 10 to 14 years, be rounded up and sold to Jamaican planters as slaves. This operation was soon expanded with over 100,000 Irish children and another 52,000 Irish women being sold as slaves to Jamaica, Antigua, and Montserrat.

The trade in Irish slaves expanded and by 1664 Irish slaves were being sold to the French on St. Bartholomen as well as other colonies. The planters in the Caribbean found that the Irish slaves were not as well suited for labor in the tropics as African slaves. The African slaves were less affected by tropical diseases than the Irish slaves.

Due to this difference and the increased costs of shipping and handling, as well as the initial purchase price from African dealers, the male African slave was worth approximately 900 pounds of cotton or 50 pounds sterling.

An Irish slave on the other hand was free for the taking in Ireland and was typically only going for 5 pounds sterling.   Due to the war in Ireland the vast majority of Irish slaves were women and children, who usually cost even less than 5 pounds sterling apiece. French, English and Spanish planters soon found a way to make a good profit from the situation. They knew that those African's who did not contract malaria would spawn children, half of which were also impervious to malaria. Today we know this was a result of them being carriers for the genetic disease called Sickle-cell-anemia.   While the planters of the 1600's didn't know why it happened, they did understand how it worked.

These planters as well as others soon initiated breeding programs. They would purchase an African male slave who had proven to be resistant to malaria and was exceptionally muscular. This African would serve as stud for the inexpensive Irish women slaves they could purchase; 50% of the offspring from this cross (the F-1 generation) were impervious to malaria and commanded top dollar as slaves.

These breeding programs worked so well that by 1681 legislation was proposed to stop this because it was reducing the profits of the Royal African Company which was importing African Slaves; however, due to the profitability of these breeding programs the practice continued until well after the end of Ireland's "Potato Famine".

Recent DNA studies of Jamaicans and other islanders found that the vast majority of the female (Maternal) X chromosomes are those of Irish women. It proves that these breeding programs did in fact establish the current populations of many Caribbean Islands and one source of slaves for the English Colonies in North America.

Ireland was the primary source for slaves to much of the "English" New World from the 1600's to early 1700's. Due to the wars in Ireland other countries also came in to take Irish people as slaves, the most notable being in 1631.

On June 20, 1631 a Moroccan fleet commanded by Morat Rais landed at the city of Baltimore in South West Ireland and took the civilian population away as slaves. Only three citizens of Baltimore ever made it back to Ireland.

After Morat Rais had sacked Baltimore he sailed to Algiers, North Africa and sold the Irish people as slaves. Several French Missionaries in Algiers witnessed the auctions of the Irish slaves but could do nothing about it, after the auctions these people were never seen again.

It should be noted that the slavery of Europeans by Muslims had gone on for a very long time and that this was not an isolated or infrequent event. Italian children are taken as slaves from costal towns by Muslim boats even today, with Italian Coast Guard ships intercepting Muslim slave catchers several times a year in the Mediterranean.

In historical contrast there were approximately 11 million African Slaves shipped across the Atlantic to the New World; of this number approximately 500,000 African's were sold to the area that is the currently United States. This amounts to about 4.4% of the total African slaves. Of the African American population in the United States today DNA results show a mixture of Maternal X chromosomes from Irish women and African women. The populations descending from these imported slaves are a significant part of the population at large.

In contrast to the 11 million African Slaves that were shipped to North and South America, there were an estimated 28 million African Slaves shipped to the Muslim Middle East. The Middle East had been taking slaves for longer and was much closer to the source.

The Middle East used African slaves as farm laborers, servants, soldiers and in particular to work mining operations. The gold mines of Wadi Al Hamat were a prime example. The area around the operations had an estimated number of burials of at least several hundred thousand. The vast majority of these graves have proven to be those of African Slaves.

Due to the extreme conditions of climate and the barbaric mining processes the life expectancy for African Slaves on these mining operations was very short.

The Muslim slave catchers typically killed the elderly and infants as well as any persons with physical or mental problems, before initiating the transportation of the slaves. The African Males were typically castrated, while any offspring of Arab masters from African females were also castrated.

The fabled Mameluke divisions fielded by the various Muslim states were composed of these castrated African males; for example, the Mameluke army that did battle with Napoleon at the Pyramids in Egypt was composed of these "expendable" shock troops.

The result is that today there are almost no descendants from the estimated 28 million African slaves taken by Muslims into the Middle East.

It should be noted that by the early 1800's Europeans began to view slavery as ethically wrong, while the Muslim's did not.

In point of fact the Koran endorses slavery and the Profit Mohammad was reported to have had numerous slaves. Of the Profit Muhammad's slaves there are the names of over forty recorded by Muslim Chroniclers.

The enslaved Africans had under Muslim states absolutely no rights, while under Christian states African slaves were required to be fed and cared for up to and including their old age (retirement).

As an example the Nation of Saudi Arabia in the Middle East did not make slavery illegal until 1962. This however should be taken with the fact that the Nation of Peru in South America did not abolish slavery until 1968.

The Location of one of the major Washoe refugee camps provided by the Maidu. Located in the serpentine belt near the intersection of Traverse Creek Road and Meadow brook Road along Traverse Creek.. Slavery caused Native peoples to move to safe areas long before Europeans arrived.

The French

The French had colonies in North America, namely Canada, Louisiana and Haiti. Haiti was a prime location for sugar production and so French landowners in Haiti began purchasing inexpensive West African female slaves from the Spanish. Malaria in Haiti made life expectancy short but for those West Africans who were carriers of Sickel-cell-anemia the disease had no effect.

French men took these West African women and the initial hybrid population was rather successful. The initial cross of a Frenchman with an African woman (who was a carrier of Cycle-cell-anemia) produced children who were immune to malaria. This population developed into a slave-holding society where the slave owners themselves were part-African, so the degree of skin color determined social status.

Emperor Napoleon the First of France

When the French Revolution declared that all people were free, the Haitian population was thrown into turmoil. The loss of revenue from Haiti was hurting France. The arrival of Napoleon soon reinstated slavery, at least on paper to Haiti.

The slaves now revolted, using a close copy of the American Constitution, and drove the slave holders from the island. These Haitian refugees were the aristocrats and well-to-do, most of them ended up in the nearby French colony of Louisiana. They became known as Creoles, as they were cultured and had some wealth they began to run plantations and businesses in Louisiana like before.

The Creoles are not to be confused with the Cajuns. The Cajuns are the descendents of families of French men who married Native American women along the Saint Lawrence River basin in Canada. This was a very productive population with prosperous farms, after the defeat of the French in the French and Indian War they were forcibly removed from their farms by the British. Brittan wanted English settlers to live along the St. Lawrence Seaway to secure the Canadian colony for Britain. These refugees went down rivers (or by ship along the coast) to the remaining French Colony of Louisiana. As a rural people they settled in the Achafalia Basin of Louisiana, Mississippi, and East Texas.

The French traders (who initially went into the Louisiana country) had intermarried with the Choctaw tribe and had fairly good relations.

In a determined effort to restore French revenue Napoleon dispatched an elite Bronze Eagle division to retake Haiti to return slavery to the island.

The Haitians were in despair as they had only a few cannon and not nearly enough muskets, let alone ammunition and trained soldiers. At this time a prominent Voodoo doctor promised deliverance from the French Army, if Haiti would believe in his magic and make the proper sacrifices.

This was done in a last ditch effort to avoid being bayoneted, as the French Generals promised they would do to all those who had led the revolt. The French force arrived in 1802 and (mysteriously) every single French Officer died of yellow fever, before they even got their army onshore. Better than 80% of the Bronze Eagle division died of yellow fever within a month and the ships returned to France with the few sickly survivors.

To the French the Haitians were in league with the devil. To the Haitians, they were delivered from certain death by their voodoo religion.

The French had seen little value in Louisiana and sold it to Spain, but when Napoleon invaded Spain the Louisiana country was returned back to French control. With the failure to retake Haiti in 1802, Napoleon was eager to get rid of Louisiana for cash, so in 1803 America purchased it; swamps, alligators, malaria, yellow fever and all. We owe this great real estate deal to a Haitian Voodoo doctor.

As a result of the French influence most groups in Louisiana were allies to the Americans in the War of 1812 against the British. In the American Civil War many Creoles served in the Confederate Army as they saw their interests being better-served if slavery continued, after the war many lost their fortunes. Post Civil War Jim Crow laws did not recognize their classification system, Mulatto; half white and half black, Quadroon; one-fourth black, Octaroon; one-eighth black or other fractions, they were simply classified as all colored. This financial and social loss was disastrous and the Creole population suffered numerous suicides and alcoholism as a result.

The American Civil War had little effect on the Cajuns as they had no vested interests either way, but after the war they were looked down on as a people of mixed blood.

Chief of the Apache Neitche was the son of Cochise and his Baca wife .The Baca family were Spanish Jews who had fled the Inquisition by moving to New Mexico. Neitche proved to be a very able leader both in war and peace.

Chief Quanah Parker of the Comanche Tribe.

Further North the offspring of Indian mothers and French trappers and traders tended to stay with their mother's people. they were called Métis. The various tribes to which the Metis were related found them to be very valuable in dealing with Europeans. They were more trusted generally as they were family by blood and yet spoke and understood the languages and culture of the Europeans.

Pictured to the left Washoe from Lake Tahoe. A friendly people who needed people who shared both cultures to help them.

My family name comes from a Métis union. A French Doctor named Joel Nixon (Nixion) was a Huguenot, a Protestant Frenchman, with the rise of Napoleon all non Catholic French were to be expelled from France.

Doctor Joel took a ship to Louisiana, once in Louisiana he went up river and eventually came to the Osage Tribe. Here he practiced medicine, vaccinating the Osage against smallpox and doing surgeries and bone-settings. He soon married an Osage women and had a Son named Yenglenka Nixon.

Yenglenka Nixon married the daughter of an American Mountain Man named Bill Williams. Bill met Acinga Redcorn of the Gross Corte Band of the Osage Tribe and they were married. Their marriage produced two daughters Mary and Sarah Williams. While Americans might call these children half-breeds they were fairly well accepted by the people originating from the Appalachians.

Both Mary and Sarah attended school in Kentucky before returning to Missouri to live with their mother's tribe. When Yenglenka Nixon married Mary Williams their first son was taken by Mary to a local German Herr Schulenmaker (who was the Catholic Priest at a mission near by) and had her child christened Bill Nixon. Since the boy also had the Osage names for his father's clan (Red Panther) and mother's family (Redcorn) he would be better able to move from one culture to the other.

Educated at the Mission school, and working in the family store he learned to speak Osage, French, English, Cherokee, Choctaw, Creek and Pawnee; as well as do algebra and some calculus in his head. He would later become a Supreme Court Judge as well as a Baptist Preacher.

My Grandfather's Grandfather a (Métis) Bill Nixon

Red Panther Bill Nixon Redcorn of the Gross Corte

Middle Rivers Band of the Great Osage Tribe

It was from the ranks of these Métis that the "Principal Chiefs" of many tribes would be elected.

Principal Chief George Washington Grayson (of the Creek Nation), Principal Chief John Ross (of the Cherokee Nation), even Chief Quanah Parker (of the Comanche) and Nietche Chief (of the Chericowa Apache) were Métis. All of them were astute intelligent people who served their tribes politically in dealing with the American Government.

George Washington Grayson
Chief of the Creek Nation

In Western Canada the Métis (from intermarriages with Cree, Ojibwa, Soulteaux, French Canadian and Scottish) became a unique society that unified it's political voice. One of the Métis leaders, Louis Riel, established the Canadian province of Manitoba. The Anglo-Canadian land companies saw him and the Métis as a threat to their business and conducted a resurvey of the land that would displace the Métis' farms. The angry Métis arrested these surveyors and held them for trial. This was used as an excuse for the Anglo Canadian forces to call this a rebellion and organized the Wolseley Expedition (authorized by Sir John A. Macdonald) to deal with the problem in 1870.

Louis Riel Leader of the Canadian Métis people.

Louis Riel and the leaders of the Canadian Métis.

Wolseley and his force broke up the Métis and forced Louis Reil into exile. Louis went across the border into Montana where he married Marguerite Bellehumeur (a Métis herself) in1881. They had three children while teaching Sioux children in a Quaker sponsored school. He was elected to the Canadian House of Commons three times but was not allowed to assume his seat.

In 1885 the Métis had reorganized and created the new Canadian Province of Saskatchewan and Louis Reil was sent for to come and represent the Métis grievances to the Canadian government. This was met with a full British Army that was marched all the way to Saskatchewan where they were defeated by the Métis several times until the Métis ran out of ammunition and were finally overrun. Louis Reil was captured and executed. In 1993 the Métis finally received recognition as a distinct culture by the Canadian government

Black slaves and Native Americans

For those tribes in the Southern United States, there was an issue of what to do with fugitive black slaves who had escaped into their Indian nations. For the Seminole, these fugitives were adopted into the tribe and made full members of their society.

General Watie

Later after many of this tribe were defeated and removed to the Indian Territory, they joined General Stand Watie in his Confederate Indian Army under Colonel John Jumper. Seminole Choctaw and Creek had the descendants of many Indian and black marriages in them. It is a misconception that black men did not serve in the Confederate Armed Forces some even as officers.

After the Civil War many black Seminole served in the US Cavalry. They got the name "Buffalo Soldiers" by the Western Indian tribes because of their curly hair. Since these men had grown up with tracking skills and woodcraft they proved invaluable to the US Army during the Western Indian wars.

Colonel John Jumper of the Seminole Tribe.

The Cherokee had a different approach to the problem. Since fugitive black slaves had nowhere to go, many Cherokee offered that if they would work on their farm for a percentage of the crop the Cherokee would draw up papers (Usually in Cherokee) that showed the slave had been bought and belonged to the Cherokee. The wealthy Cherokee also purchased black slaves, often at the direction of their own "slaves" and thus reunited black families. As a point in fact, the terms of Cherokee slavery were much better than their white counterparts; for example they could own guns and personal property, to such a degree that after the Civil War the Cherokees' slaves continued to live with them and considered themselves part of Cherokee society.

The Geo-Politics of the American Civil War and the Emancipation Proclamation.

It is taken for granted that the reason for the American Civil War was the issue of slavery. While it was clearly an issue, there were many other issues and the actual Emancipation Proclamation was given as a result of a foreign threat more than as an act of benevolence.

The start of the American Civil War was seen by the European powers as a "Golden Opportunity". As fast as the news reached Europe that the war had started the European powers met. By October of 1861 at the Treaty of London Great Britain, Spain and France united to set up an invasion force to take Mexico. They had some Mexican monarchists as well as the Upper Class of the Catholic Church in Mexico who were willing to accept a foreign monarch being put in power over Mexico.

The European powers settled on Archduke Ferdinand Maximilian Joseph of Austria.

Maximilian was a brother to Emperor Franz Joseph of Austria, who would be leading the Austro-Hungarian Empire into World War One.

Maximilian was the result of an affair between Sophie Friederike, Princess of Bavaria, and Napoleon the II.

Empress Maria Eugenia Armijo

Emperor Napoleon III of France

Since every member of the royal families of Europe knew this, he was an embarrassment.

Also Maximilian had contracted a sexually-transmitted disease that had rendered him sterile. As such, he was the perfect monarch to place on the Mexican throne.

By January 1862 French troops were landing in Mexico. Their orders from Napoleon the III, a half brother to Maximilian, were that French forces would secure the Mexican silver mines. Once these mines were secured the forces could then take the presidential palace in Mexico City. The French forces where authorized to use as many "prisoners of war" as necessary to operate the silver and "quick-silver" (Mercury) mines. The Catholic church also owned many mines and these were allowed full access to the "prisoners of war" to run their mining operations as well.

Emperior Maximilian and his wife Carlota sister of King Leopold II

In the Occupation of Mexico the American Monroe Doctrine was ignored, and while the U.S.A. and C.S.A. protested this invasion, they were ignored by France, England and Spain.

Britain for her part began to send more troops numbering nearly 80,000 to garrison their Canadian forts along the border with the Northern U.S.

It was only after massive defeats of the Union forces at the hands of the Confederacy that negotiations started which would recognize the Confederate States as the dominant "America" by Britain. In response President Lincoln made his Emancipation Proclamation.

King Leopold II of Belgium Brother of Carlota

French Marshal Francios-Acille

This proclamation would make a British invasion of the Northern U.S. look as though Britain supported the cause of slavery.

Britain had been politically against slavery since 1808 and, while they might profit by other countries' use of slaves, they could not be seen politically to be supportive of the institution.

This was a master-stroke by Lincoln, as he could now take Union forces positioned along the Canadian border and send them South for battles against the Confederacy. It should be noted that if the abolition of slavery was the primary goal of the Union cause, it should have been stated at the beginning of the war. Also the Emancipation Proclamation itself only emancipated slaves living in Confederate states. Those slaves living in Washington D.C. and other Union held areas were to remain in slavery per this proclamation.

Realizing the actions by the European powers to take advantage of the American Civil War, shows what they were willing to do with the situation faced by California a mere decade earlier.

Presidente Benito Juarez of Mexico was a Zapotec Indian, the first Native American leader of a nation in the Western Hemisphere after European Colonization. He had had enough of European Powers meddling in the internal affairs of Mexico (and made a point of it) by having Emperor Maximilian shot.

The Second Mexican Empire   (Imperio Mexico)

As it pertains to the institution of slavery in Western North America, the people and motivations behind the occupation of Mexico by European powers from 1862 –1867 deserves more attention.

Few Americans and even fewer Mexicans realize the scope and ramifications of the Second Mexican Empire under Emperor Maximilian.

Mexico had won independence in 1821 and by 1822 established itself as the First Mexican Empire under Augustine de Iturbide as the Emperor. This was overthrown in 1823 followed by more revolutions and counter revolutions. Mexico vacillated between being a Republic and a Dictatorship. Initially the new nation of Mexico was under the rule of Emperor Augustine de Iturbide who recognized the Church's vast land holdings but subsequent presidents and dictators had plans that retained or took away some if not all of the churches lands and silver mines as a way to encourage economic growth.

The primary Dictator during this period was General Antonio Lopez de Santa Anna who by military revolts took the post of Dictator of Mexico 11 TIMES !!! While it is true that Presidente Vicente Guerrero abolished the slavery of Africans in Mexico in 1828. Generalisimo Santa Anna would capitalize on the Mexican Army's source of income from selling Mayans taken in the Yucatan as slaves by authorizing full scale marketing of them to Cuba in 1854.

While most Americans are aware of the Texas Revolution against Santa Anna, almost none are aware that this was only the third revolt in that Mexican province. The Yucatan declared independence from Mexico in 1838 and while put down repeatedly, revolted yet again and again for a total of three times by 1845. The Mayans were being supplied with guns, ammunition and other military supplies by the British from their colony of Belize.

The various Mexican States and independence movements

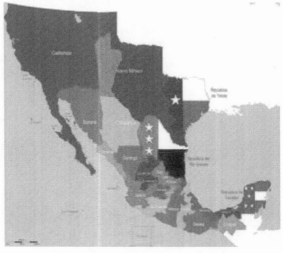

While this was sanctioned from London as part of Britain's war against slavery and was seen as a noble cause against the very Cuban slave traders that Britain had defeated off the coast of Africa back in 1827. The Mayans were paying for it by providing the British with prime stands of timber. The British viewed the Mayans as being more politically stable than Mexico and they paid their bills, so it was in Britians interest that an independent Yucatan be formed. The Mayan resistance and struggle for independence continued in a war called the Caste War when the French invaded Mexico in 1862. For the Mayan people the French were no different than the Mexicans and the war continued.

In this series of revolutions Santa Anna had managed to negotiate a large loan from the Catholic Church by promising that Catholicism would be the state religion of Mexico. He then used this money to purchase military surplus arms, artillery and even uniforms of the late Emperor Napoleon Bonaparte's French Army. It was with these arms and equipment that he put down several revolutions in Mexico before taking on the Texans and being defeated.

Now I need to insert a cast of characters which include three sons of Emperor Napoleon II, the oldest nephew of Emperor Napoleon Bonaparte.

The first is Duc de Morny who was the largest single holder of Mexican bonds. He was very upset when Mexican Presidente Juarez placed a moratorium on repaying the 80 million pesos in foreign debt. Presidente Juarez was in a hard place as Mexican politicians had embezzled vast amounts of money and he would bankrupt his country if he turned over 80 million pesos to the foreign creditors.

Duc de Morny

However Duc de Morny was not as helpless as the other British, French and Spanish investors, he had a half brother, Emperor Napoleon III of France. For his own part Napoleon III was motivated not only by his half brother but also his wife Empress Maria Eugenia Armijo was the daughter of the King of Spain, her sister Isabella II was now the Queen of Spain and they were very interested in taking Mexico back under their control.

The sisters were not only being encouraged by Duc de Morny or the other investors but by the Catholic Church, which was very interested in regaining access to their holdings in Mexico.

This coalesced in the Tripartide Agreement in London between Great Britain, France and Spain that IF hostilities were to break out in the United States, thus disabling the Americans from enforcing their Monroe Doctrine, they would invade Mexico and reestablish the monarchy there.

The question for the royal families was who to put on the throne of Mexico. Now insert another son of Napoleon II. All the royal familles realized that the Princess of Bavaria Mary and wife of Franz Joseph I, Emperor of the Austro-Hungarian Empire, had an affair with Napoleon II and that her first son Maximilian didn't look anything like her husband Franz Joseph I or her second son Franz Joseph II, and this was an embarrassment.

Queen Isabella II of Spain sister of Maria Eugenia Armijo

Maximilian had married Carlota daughter of King Leopold I and Princess of Belgium. It was well known that the couple suffered from at least two venereal diseases that had rendered them infertile. In an effort to make the best of the situation Franz Joseph I of the Austro-Hungarian Empire stripped Maximilian of the right of succession to the throne of the Austro-Hungarian

Napoleon II nephew of Napoleon Bonaparte

Empire and gave it to his son Franz Joseph II, but offered Maximilian the throne of Mexico. In this way the royal families of Europe could get Max and Carlota out of their embarrassing social dilemma and if the Mexican throne was stabilized there wouldn't be any heirs and a more suitable monarch could be selected when Max and Carlota passed away, which due to their disease was seen as being at most decade away.

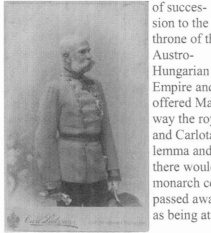

Emperor Franz Joseph

Troops were needed to invade Mexico but the

military intelligence indicated that Prussia was preparing to have a war with Austria and France, it was only a question of when. This information proved true as the Austro-Prussian War would start in 1866 and the Franco – Prussian War would start in 1868.

With these concerns the French decided to use Sudanese Muslim Soldiers and Algerian Native French Foreign Legion troops under French and Austrian Officers in their invasion of Mexico. While there were some units that were made up of European soldiers, the few that were deployed initially were nearly all replaced with African troops once the hostilities in Europe began.

These African forces were called Zuavo by the Mexicans and Chasseurs d Afrique Corps by the French and Austrians. For Princess Carlota her brother King Leopold II, now King of Belgium sent a special force known as The Regiment of Empress Carlota, made up of African troops from his colony in the Congo, under Belgian officers.

Zuavos and Chasseurs d Afrique Corps

Many of the Austrian officers were of Polish, Hungarian and Bohemian decent and the majority had experience putting down Polish peasant revolts in Europe.

The Austro-Belgian force started with 2,000 men while the French– Austrian force was nearly 35,000 men. After the landings in Vera Cruz these forces were augmented by Mexican hacendadoes and Mexican Nobility as well as a few mercenaries.

Napoleon III

The Supreme Commander of the Occupying Forces was French Marshal Francois-Achille Bazaine. From the start the order was that troops could confiscate all property of those who took up arms against the French and had not immediately surrendered. This was later expanded to what became known as the Black Decree, signed by Emperor Maximilian himself, which allowed captured guerillas (and by logical extension any Mexican) to be shot on sight or captured and sold as a slave.

The real problem for the European officers was that their Zuavo (African Troops) were motivated by the opportunity to rape without consequence. Many young Mexican women died at the hands of the Zuavos and more still were impregnated by them.

While Presidente Vicente Guerrero had been a mulatto (part African) himself, there were very few people in Mexico with any African ancestry. In order to make it socially easier for the offspring of these Zuavos in Mexican society they were claimed to be the offspring of escaped African-American Slaves. In reality few American slaves ever tried to escape South across the forbidding South Texas Desert and fewer still actually made it. The region in Southern Texas was too dry to support large agricultural operations and as such had very few slaves in the first place. In addition the Mexican bandits who roamed the border were more than eager to capture escaped American Slaves which they could then sell.

It is now realized that the bulk of the African-Mexican population is the result of the French Occupation from 1862– 1867.

The Occupation also drew a rarely understood group of mercenaries to join the forces of Porifero Diaz.

One group was lead by Luis Ghilardi, he lead a group of Italians who wanted to fight the Austro-Hungarian Empire. They served the Mexican Republic very well but when Luis Ghilardi was captured he was summarily shot.

Another group of mercenaries was the American Legion of Honor lead by Colonel George Mason Green as well as Lew Wallace and former General George Church. They recruited men for the Legion in San Francisco, California and held fund raising banquets. Some records indicate they might have raised as many as 6,000 men for the legion and served Porfirero Dias so well that they were put in the Victory Parade in Mexico City by Presidente Porifero Diaz. The majority of the Legion of Honor men from California were German emigrants who wanted to fight the French. The rest of the men as well as some of the Germans felt that they should support Republican governments and were against Absolute Monarchies.

Another interesting incident started as Colonel Edelmiro Mayer, the Commanding officer of the 7th US Colored Infantry, was stationed along the US Mexican border in Texas. Edelmiro was fluent in German and was able to understand the orders and comments from the Austrian Officer in command of a unit of Maximilians Zuavo's. With out orders Edelmiro lead his 7th Colored Infantry across the Rio Grande and attacked the Austrian Officer and his command defeating them to the relief of the local Mexican population. For his actions Edelmiro was praised by Porifero Diaz and was not reprimanded by the US Government.

Following this incident numerous shipments of surplus American Civil War arms ammunition and cannon were delivered to the Mexican Republican forces from the US Government.

For the Catholic Church Nobility the defeat of Maximilian's forces in Northern Mexico caused them to negotiate the transfer of a considerable amount of money (the amount varies) to the care of Texas Governor Andrew J Hamilton. That the Catholic Church of Mexico would entrust their money to an American, Texas Governor who was a Baptist for safe keeping shows the strange situation in which they found themselves. However, Andrew J. Hamilton was good to his word and he did keep the Churches money safe until they asked for it's return several years later. In researching the Mexican Catholic Churches reasoning for the Texas Governor to keep their money safe was because they wanted the money to start the operation of their silver mines again once the hostilities had finished.

The Mexican Troops of General Diaz at the firing squad of Maximilian.

Durring his reign as Emperor of Mexico Maximilian did one thing that truly upset the royalty of Europe, he officially adopted the two Grandsons of the First Emperor of Mexico Augustin de Iturbide, Don Agustin and Don Salvados. As a result of this action the current pretender t the throne of Mexico is Maximilian von Gotzon-Itrubide.

As the regime fell and Maximilian was captured his half Brother Franz Joseph II reinstated Maximillians right to the throne of the Austro-Hungarian Empire and asked the American Secretary of State to intervene on behalf of his brother. The US State department responded that as Maximilian was never the recognized leader of the Mexican people there was nothing they would do.

Emperor Maximilian of Mexico was the disposable monarch placed on the new throne by Europe's monarchs, who was in the end disposed of by General Juarez.

Pictured above French Foreign Legion Troops in Mexico under Maximilian

After Maximilian was killed by firing squad Franz Joseph wanted his brothers corps returned. Mexico insisted that Franz Joseph II would need to officially recognize their country and write a personnel letter asking for the return of his brothers corps. Franz Joseph II did this and Mexico did return his brothers body. As an historical note Mexico was the only country to officially object to the German occupation of Austria in 1938 and so today in Vienna there is a park called Mexikoplatz to honor this action.

An interesting refugee from Mexico after the fall of the French Occupation was Father Roccatani, Antonio de la Kosa, he showed up in Belgium and Austria with a proposal for King Leopold and Emperor Franz Joseph, he would give them the Mexican formula for converting silver into gold for the reasonable price of only 5 million silver florin. They actually paid the GOOD FATHER several thousand silver florin before the scam was reavled!!!

The Prince Imperial died at the hands of the Zulu.

As it turned out all three of Napoleon II's sons would soon die. After Maximilian was shot by order of Porfiero Diaz, France lost the Franco– Prussian War by 1871 and Emperor Napoleon III was removed only to die and his wife and son went into exile, the last son Duc de Morny died in 1877.

These deaths left The Prince Imperial, Emperor Napoleon III's only son as the last of Napoleon Bonapart's royal line. Then while serving with the British Army the Prince Imperial managed to get himself killed by a Zulu's spear in 1879 Durring the Zulu War of South Africa.

Pictured above is a Chasseurs d Afrique in Mexico.

This animosity by European Monarchs toward the US prevailed long after the French Occupation of Mexico in the Second Mexican Empire.

A prime example was the German Kaiser's Operational Plan 3, created in 1903 for the planned invasion of the United States using 60 ships and over 100,000 men. The plan involved shelling New York City and the capture of Boston.

The Kaiser did not like the United States and believed that it would crumble if it were to suffer even a modest attack on several of its larger cities along the East Coast.

The Kaiser also had plans for the capture of Puerto Rico and the Panama Canal . While the Germans never did put these plans into action this is another example of the European leaders mindset of the period.

It should be noted that it was only American President Theodore Roosevelt who made the Kaiser uneasy and made him begin to doubt his impression of American vulnerability.

California and the Contenders
for Control.

Although discovered early on, California had been a backwater of the Spanish Empire. It was left alone until Russian fur trappers and the Vitus Bering Expedition of Tsarist Russia explored the coast in 1741.

This alarmed Spain's King Phillip V, prompting him to have more exploration of the region. The news of the Russians establishing forts down the coast motivated the King of Spain to secure this part of the Spanish Empire. While Spain needed a string of forts along the coast as a bare minimum, to do so directly would anger the Russians. This could bring about bigger problems for the Spanish as their shipping of goods from their colony in the Philippines around the Pacific necessitated stopovers in the Russian ports of Vladivostok and Sitka Alaska.

Pictured above Mexican Governor of California General Mariano G. Vallejo.

To do what he needed and yet not anger the Russians King Charles III of Spain decided in 1768 that the objective was to bring Christianity to the native Indians of California. To do this a string of missions along California's coast was proposed, each with a Presidio (fort) nearby to protect the mission from hostile Indians. Note, that the Presidios were usually positioned with their cannon pointing toward the sea (not the land) and you can tell what the real purpose of the Mission project was.

The Tsarist Russian Fort Ross In California

The first Mission in Alta California at San Diego was established in 1769. Spanish arrogance and their expectation that the native Kumeyaay tribe should provide them with food, labor and submit themselves to Catholic and Spanish rules and authority resulted in 800 warriors, on the 4th of November 1775 destroying the mission and taking their food back from these "free loading Spanish ingrates".

California from the Natives point of view.

Spanish immigration to California was minimal at best and to get a population into California loyal to Spain required giving them free reign. Spanish Dons were given huge tracts of land that they could operate with little if any interference from the Spanish government. For example Don Joaquin de Estrada had 70,000 acres of land with 12,000 head of cattle and 4,000 horses. If a Don wished to use Indians as slaves nobody was going to interfere.

With Napoleon Bonaparte's invasion of Spain and the placing his brother on the Spanish throne, it was inevitable that many Spanish colonies would gain their independence, including Mexico. Spain simply lacked the forces necessary to hold on to all of it's empire.

For the next several decades Mexico was torn by revolution after revolution. (While I could not get a statistic for 1849 I do have one for 1877.) By 1877 Mexico had been a republic for a little over 50 years and the office of the Presidente had changed 70 times. The Mexican State of Chihuahua had gone through 82 administrations during this same period. Roving gangs of "banditos" would occupy whole towns and "tax" them for extended periods of time. These gangs would take over silver mines and run them using the local population, especially "indios", as slave labor. The large ranchos had their own private armies to drive the banditos off their lands, or silver mines, and for use in joining revolutions.

California was now a State of Mexico and Governor General Marino G. Vallejo was burdened with many problems. He was an extremely intelligent man who unlike most others was trying to do the best for "his people", the citizens of California. With the chaos and corruption in the rest of Mexico it was a foregone conclusion that California would eventually come under some other authority. Governor Vallejo intended to steer his "state" into the best option available.

The Contenders

There were five contenders for California; the Russians, the Spanish, the English, the Mormons and the Americans.

The Russians claimed Northern California and had built a fort along the coast. Fort Ross was intended to support their claim and (more importantly) to provide food for the Russians' Alaskan Colony. The Russians had tried growing wheat and barley but the humidity had caused the crops to rot. An enterprising Ukrainian living at Fort Ross had an idea. The local Russian River ran an enormous quantity of carp. While as fish species go carp is about as inedible as they come, they could be used as feed for pigs. The pigs could be processed with the meat cured and smoked, providing food for the Russians' Alaskan colony.

The problem the Russians faced was that they didn't have any pigs. They could go North to the British colony in Seattle and buy pigs, but that would reveal their vulnerability. They could go South to the Mexicans but again, that would show their state of vulnerability. They went instead to the Southernmost tip of their possessions on the Kamchatka Peninsula in Siberia just North of Japan, and captured wild hogs. These were put in pens at Fort Ross and fed carp. The wild hogs tore up the pens and ran off into the forests of Northern California.

In a 1995 DNA analysis of the wild pigs in Sonoma County California revealed them to be Japanese Wild Boar. This was a surprise to the California Department of Fish and Game until the history of the Russians at Fort Ross was revealed and confirmed by the Russian records.

With the complete lack of success at Fort Ross the Tsarist Russian Empire was not very interested in expanding their empire along the Pacific Rim. The Russian victories along the river Volga had opened up the Black Sea, so now Russia was concentrating troops in an effort to get the Turks to allow them access to the Mediterranean Sea. A warm-water trade route to the heart of Europe was far more valuable to Russia than another unprofitable colony on the other side of the world.

Spain

Spain was beginning to recover from the Napoleonic Wars and had managed to retain it's colony in the Philippines. This despite a Jihad from Moslems (Moros) in the Southern Philippines based in (Mindanao). This required more and more Spanish Troops to maintain control. It was possible that California might wish to return to the stability of Spain; however an invasion force would be hard to supply and probably lose if they encountered any more than token resistance. With this in mind, Spanish agents were sent to get a feel for Governor Vallejo's disposition about a return to Spanish control of California.

England

The British Empire stretched across the Northern part of the continent and California would be a nice addition to the empire. Britain was extremely eager to contain the Americans and having been Spain's ally in driving Napoleon from Spain, believed they could get Spain's support if they took California. Britain had recognized the property rights of the Spanish landlords after the removal of Napoleon from Spain and they would do the same in California. World events would give the British Empire more difficulty in California than was first assessed.

The first problem was China. The Chinese governments were becoming increasingly hostile to the British for selling opium to their people. So when the Chinese seized the East India Company Island of their coast and burned 2.6 million pounds of opium and seized another 26000 chests of opium the company decided to try to seize enough Chinese goods to make good these losses. This started the First Opium War in 1839.The East India Trading Company was unable to provide enough Company troops to keep their operations open in China and additional Crown troops were required. From 1839 until 1842 Crown troops fought Chinese authorities to keep the East India Trading Company's opium markets open.

British troops fighting in Canton against Chinese authorities, who didn't want the British selling drugs to their citizens during the First Opium War in 1841.

Even after 1842 things were simmering until the Second Opium War (Anglo-Chinese War) broke out in 1856, lasting until 1860.

During the 1840's more and more Crown troops were being stationed in China and were unavailable for use in California.

Another issue for England was their Colony of India. The Sepoy people of India were becoming increasingly irritated at the actions of the East India Trading Company, this demanded additional British Crown troops to maintain order. This would eventually blow up into the Indian Revolt or Sepoy Mutiny.

The last of the problems facing a potential British invasion of California was Southern Africa. During the Napoleonic Wars a Dutch Colony on the South African Cape was acquired by the British. This colony was absolutely necessary for re-supplying ships bound to and from England, India and China.

The Zulu Tribe of Southern Africa, had in 1816 only occupied an area of only 10 square miles. By 1839 under the command of Chaka, the Zulu had expanded to an area larger than that of England, France and Germany combined.

At this point another figure comes into the story. The Portuguese Governor of Goa at this time was Bernardo De Silva who happened to be the first and only Governor of Goa's 451 years of existence to be of native India Indian ancestry. Bernardo was appalled at the British East India Company taking over more and more small independent Indian states in their rush to increase their opium production. While Bernardo knew he had neither the troops or resources to confront the British in India proper he did have an idea. As the Portuguese Governor of (Goa) in Western India he also had authority over the Portuguese Colonies located in South East Africa (later called Mozambique), which he now authorized to begin selling guns to the Zulu. The Zulu armies were estimated at more than 250,000 men and once armed with guns they could easily take the English Colony of Natal. This meant ever greater numbers of Crown troops would be needed in the South African Cape making them unavailable for service in India..

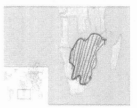

The size of the new Zulu Empire in South Africa was now being armed by the Portuguese from Mozambique.

If Chaka Zulu not been born it is quite possible that California would have become a British province. Few realize the American West did not exist in a vacuum, that international Geopolitics affected the lives of even the most remote populations of Native Americans.

These conflicts put a tremendous strain on the professional army of the British Empire; since their army was a completely volunteer force they simply couldn't increase their troop strength by drafting men. As enticing as California was it would have to be taken with minimal force and if possible with the help of the Governor Vallejo himself. British agents were sent to feel out Governor Vallejo to see if he would be willing to accept a British takeover of the state.

The Mormons

Brigham Young

California was also being considered the natural seaport for the new Mormon State of Deseret. Brigham Young sent Mormon units forward into California to test out the possibility of taking the area into the new Mormon state. One group was working for John Sutter on a sawmill in Coloma under James Marshal. The Mormons were nominally sent to California to work, the discovery of gold at Sutters Mill would change the whole equation but I'll get into that later. The idea of the Mormon state including California was even proposed by the President of the United States, Zachery Taylor. By having both areas become one state it would keep the balance of Slave and free states in the union. Zachery Taylor sent his agent John Wilson Westward with a proposal to do just this in 1849.

Brigham Young envisioned an independent Mormon State, not exactly what President Taylor had in mind. Young's desire for this independent state would explode by 1857 in the Mormon War (also known as Buchanan's Blunder)

President of the United States James Buchanan was not about to let Brigham Young and the Mormons separate from the Union! At the head of the Union Army to bring the Mormons back into the Union, was Colonel Albert Sidney

Colonel Albert S. Johnson

Later a Confederate General.

Brigham Young's vision of a Mormon Nation in Western North America

■ *State of Deseret (proposed)*

Utah Territory 1851

Johnston. In this conflict the idea of an independent Mormon state died.

The United States of America

The U.S. wanted to expand their country from coast to coast. The Louisiana Purchase gave the US most of the land necessary to reach the Pacific Coast; California was clearly a possible extension of this objective.

Governor Vallejo had pretty well narrowed down the contenders to be either the British or the Americans. The state would go to whoever made the first move and could back it up.

Now, factor in the New Idra and New Almaden cinnabar deposits located just South of San Jose California. This area has the richest Cinnabar deposits in the world. Cinnabar once processed and distilled makes Mercury, referred to in those days as "quick silver". In the 1840's the demand for mercury had exploded. In refining gold and silver, the last stage of recovery was done by running the enriched ore over copper plates coated in mercury. The waste material would float on the mercury while the gold and silver would sink into it. The mercury was then scraped off the copper plates and heated to the boiling point of mercury, driving off the mercury and leaving the gold and silver behind. Efforts were made to recover the mercury especially since it was so expensive, but the demand was outgrowing the supply.

Mercury was also an essential part of the new percussion ignition systems. This was revolutionizing the weapons systems of armies world wide and made these mines of strategic value to the British Empire. New torpedoes and artillery shells were developed by the Royal Navy that utilized this new percussion ignition. Mercury was also used in the manufacture of many domestic items, from medicines to cure bacterial infections to felt hats. The demand was growing exponentially, causing the price to skyrocket.

The process of recovering mercury from the cinnabar ore was basic but required the consumption of large amounts of firewood to fuel the ovens. The sulfur was driven off the ore and the poisonous mercury vaporized. Then it was distilled through a cooling pipe returning it to a pure liquid form that would drip into collection vessels. This refined mercury was then transferred to iron flasks for transport.

Some of these facilities were visited by the US Geological Survey Team in 1861. The journal of Mr. Brewer, a member of the team, was compiled into a book titled "Up and Down California 1861-1864".

Mr. Brewer wrote about these mercury mines in detail. One of the facts he noted was that any miner who worked in the mercury recovery ovens would eventually die if exposed for as little as four days. They might live for a month or less but exposure to the mercury in the recovery facility would lead to certain death.

This work was not particularly hard or complicated. By 1861 the labor needed to do this work came primarily from people who did not see that they had much of a future. Men with tuberculosis or severe infections could work

AN 1863 PHOTO shows the New Almaden Mine in the Santa Clara hills. The buildings with smokestacks are the smelters where the silver ore was cooked to release the mercury.

for two days and make a small fortune, which they would often spend on alcohol and ladies. These workers often had contracts so that their last wages would be sent back to family or friends. In 1861, even with wide-spread recruiting, finding laborers for this work was extremely difficult.

The ownership of the land on which these deposits were located was very questionable even in 1861. The Spanish Land Grants were primarily for the valley bottoms while these deposits were in the hills. Some mines were being sued by the owners of Spanish land claims whose nearest boundary was fifteen miles or more away. Everybody wanted a piece of the money being made in these operations. There was evidence of numerous small operations all around these deposits that had been worked in the previous decades.

Prior sources of labor

In the journals and reports I have found that mentioned the subject, both before and in the early part of the California Gold Rush, they commented on numerous Indian women and little children being sold as slaves but very few adult males. The large ranchos often bought these people for agricultural labor while many 49'ers took Indian women as wives. Many white women bought Indian children to help them with domestic chores. The presence of these women and children was rarely thought about, but several of the women who purchased Indian children commented that they must have survived diseases like smallpox or measles that had killed off the adults, particularly the men and elderly.

There are two problems with this explanation; first, when smallpox hit the Blackfeet tribe, it killed nearly all the women and children, the primary survivors were adult males. When measles went through the Piute in Northern Nevada and Southern Oregon it decimated the children not the adults. In hunter gather societies the lowest disease vector is for the adult males who are by the nature of hunting not in close contact with numerous people and thus have less exposure to disease.

It is highly improbable that diseases such as measles and smallpox would act entirely different in California's Indian populations than they did on other Western Tribes or Europeans.

Second, the other problem with this reasoning is the pictures of these children, none of them had the telltale facial scars associated with having survived smallpox. So where did these people come from? For those few Anglo-Europeans who actually asked the Indians, their story was they had been taken as slaves from their villages. So what was happening?

California prior to the coming of the Europeans.

California had practiced slavery before the coming of the Europeans but it was limited for economic reasons. The largest concentrations of slaves were in the coastal salmon-based tribes extending from central California's coast up into Alaska. Slaves in these permanent villages were used for processing salmon. Their society was probably more like that of the Spartans in ancient Greece.

A prime example of a California tribe was the Klamath. They practiced slavery in the lower reaches of their settlements along the Klamath river. Over the eons, members of the tribe who lived upstream and inland came to depend on the food supplies they could get by trading slaves down river; this part of the Klamath Tribe eventually became known as the Modoc. They began to go further and further into the interior in their search for slaves. The Modoc's source for slaves were primarily Piute, Shoshone, Bannock, Washoe, Yana and Yahi. Upon arriving with new slaves the Modoc were treated to a party of sorts with feasting and gift-giving. These were commonly called a "Potlatch".

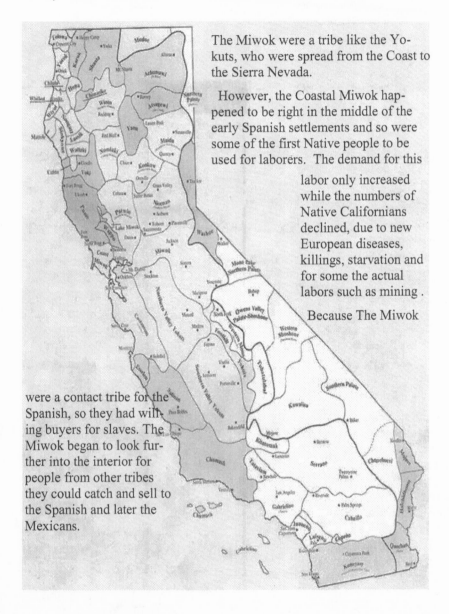

The Miwok were a tribe like the Yokuts, who were spread from the Coast to the Sierra Nevada.

However, the Coastal Miwok happened to be right in the middle of the early Spanish settlements and so were some of the first Native people to be used for laborers. The demand for this labor only increased while the numbers of Native Californians declined, due to new European diseases, killings, starvation and for some the actual labors such as mining .

Because The Miwok were a contact tribe for the Spanish, so they had willing buyers for slaves. The Miwok began to look further into the interior for people from other tribes they could catch and sell to the Spanish and later the Mexicans.

Not that all Potlatches were connected to the arrival of slaves. It was just the name for a party or celebration.

The arrival of the Russians and later other nations brought about an incentive to increase the production of dried and smoked salmon, this fueled an increase in the demand for slaves. For the Klamath with their Modoc suppliers, the slave population increased to nearly 85% by 1865 when their slaves were liberated by Abraham Lincoln's Emancipation proclamation.

Fueled by liquor and a desire to demonstrate their wealth, several Potlatches were on record as having slaves killed during the festivities, simply to demonstrate the wealth of the masters. For the Miwok Tribe there were three primary groups, Coastal, Plains and Sierra Nevada Miwok. The Miwok living along the Coast, who operated much the same as the Klamath, did practice slavery.

The inland Miwok saw no economic use for slaves themselves, but would bring slaves to their coastal relations in trade for salt, salmon and other goods.

The arrival of the Spanish brought new trade goods such as metal knives, horses and alcohol to exchange for slaves. The missions needed labor and the Ranchos even more. While the Spanish did manage to capture some Indians themselves the majority were purchased from other Indians. The labor for the mercury mines consumed a great number of these Indian men.

Slaves, with no idea what would happen to them, were used. Once they died, the bodies were simply put in the ovens along with the firewood for the next run, thus eliminating any evidence for the next group of slaves to see.

The wood necessary to run these ovens would soon denude the surrounding area and the little operation would have be abandoned, moving to another area with available wood and the operation resumed.

The Situation among the Native Tribes in El Dorado, Placer and Amador Counties.

Native Americans arrived in the Sierra Nevada foothills and hunted such exotic species as mastodons, giant sloth and Volkswagen-sized armadillos. Mastodon bones have been found with obsidian atlatal points in them. A cave just upstream of the Highway 49 crossing of the North Fork of the American River, between the towns of Cool and Auburn, had the remains of the Volkswagen-sized armadillos, mastodon teeth, the jaw of a long horned bison (believed to have been brought in by humans) and numerous skulls of California Smiledons and dire wolves. An exhibit about this cave and replicas of these fossils can be found in the bottom level of the Placer County Courthouse in Auburn, California.

The earliest human campfires revealed tribes were burning yellow pine, indicating a climate similar to today's. Later sites show the climate changed to a redwood and Douglas fir climate similar to Oregon, but a drying period had returned the area to Yellow Pine species for the most recent 2,000 years.

During the time the Native Americans lived in this region they discovered and cultivated a number of plants which they used for medicine, soap, clothing and food. Examples of local medicinal plants; Soapweed used for Poison Oak skin rash; California Coffee berry, the bark was boiled and the water used as a laxative; Yerba Santa (sainted herb) leaves were chewed to relieve pollen allergies; Willow leaves were boiled to make a tea (containing salicylic acid found in aspirin) used for pain relief and Bay leaves crushed and fumes inhaled to clear sinuses and reduce headaches.

The tribe known as Maidu or Nisenan, lived North of the South Fork of the American River. Their names are a bit of a misnomer as Maidu is an interpretation of their word for man and "nisenan" is their word for people. In the late 1700's the tribe numbered an estimated 10,000 individuals. This was probably lower than it had been in the 1400's. Maidu tradition tells that they once lived in the Sacramento Valley. A great flood of water came and nearly everyone perished. Then a great raft was seen floating around the Buttes. The valley was completely covered in one great sea. After nine days the Creator caused the mountains to part, letting the water rush back into the ocean.

This is confirmed by a Spanish ship captain who was exploring the coast of California in the early 1500's. He noted heavy snow along the beaches of Monterey County. Then came a very warm rain that dropped an enormous amount of water. He sailed into San Francisco Bay and up into what he described as a "large inland sea". He sailed around an island that (by his calculations in latitude and longitude) could only be the Marysville Buttes. It would seem that the Maidu saw his ship and described it as the "great raft".

The combination of heavy snow forcing the native people and game animals to the valley floor followed by a flood forcing them back into the snow, was the worst possible combination . This disaster and the famine following it, decimated the Native populations throughout northern and central California. Later missionaries commented on the lack of warfare between the native tribes and attributed it to the abundance of food. In point of fact they were observing a recovering population only a few generations removed from a cataclysmic disaster.

The Maidu and Miwok are a highly intelligent people, for which they are rarely given credit. The Maidu and Miwok shared several technologies that would surprise us. Europeans tended to believe that any society that was not using copper or iron was inferior and must lack intelligence. In actuality every population has its share of highly intelligent people.

Just because the Native Californians lived in a way that was less disruptive to indigenous wildlife does not make them less "civilized" than any other race of people.

The Size and Magnitude of the Sacramento and San Juaquin Valley Flood of 1543

My father Bill Nixon was working for the United States Bureau of Reclamation and was researching historic materials relating to weather patterns in California. The project was trying to determine the size of a one thousand year flood. If they could determine the size and frequency of large water events then this information would go into the design of dams and flood control structures.

My dad was looking at an English translation of the Coleccion de Documentos "Para La Historia de de Espana" and the "Coleccion de documentos de Indas" by Antonio de Herrera. This work was written about the Spanish Expedition initially led by Juan Rodriguez Cabrillo and finished by Bartolome Ferrelo from 1542 to 1543 (up the coast of California and Oregon.) The official report of this expedition was lost but a summary of the expedition was made by Andres de Urdaneta who had access to the ships logs and charts. It was Urdaneta's work that Herrera published in the 1600's that was translated to English that my father was reading.

My dad found the paper fascinating and told me to come in and "Listen to this". I was in High School at the time but the story fascinated me.

As the story went Juan Cabrillo was a Portuguese man who came to work for Hernando Cortez in Mexico (Then called New Spain). He was later involved in gold mining in Guatemala, making him very wealthy.

In 1539 the new Viceroy of New Spain commissioned Juan Cabrillo to lead an expedition up the Pacific Coast with several goals, one was to find trade opportunities and possibly a way to China. The other was to look for the Pacific end of the "North West Passage" which they believed connected Hudson's Bay with the Pacific, the Spanish called this myth the Strait of Anian.

Cabrillo had three ships built in Acajutla on the Pacific coast of El Salvador. His flagship was the 200-ton San Salvador, then a 100 ton ship the La Victoria and last a "Fragata" named San Miguel.

The fleet was provisioned and left civilization at the town of Navidad on June 27, 1542. They went up the Pacific side of Baja California and eventually to Northern California. Then the commander Juan Cabrillo broke his leg which turned gangrenous and killed him.

His navigator Bartolome Ferrelo, who was also Portuguese named Bartolome Ferrelo was named his successor and took command.

Bartolome Ferrelo then continued the expedition. He was very impressed with the anchorage of Monterey and was able to re-supply his fleet before going North. He explored the coast and probably got as far North as the Rogue River in Oregon before finally turning back. The instruments of the time gave these explorers rather accurate Latitudes but they could only guess at the longitudes as they weren't sure just how big around the Earth was.

However, what caught my father's attention was the detailed weather account. Bartolome Ferrelo was noting heavy snow depths all the way down to the beachs in Monterey. For those of us living in California today the idea of snow on the beach in Monterey is inconceivable.

Bartolome then noted that a very warm storm came in with heavy rain that lasted for two weeks or more. As he explored to the North he found a bay that lead to a large inland sea. As this might be the Pacific end of the "North West Passage" it was clearly an objective of the mission to explore this possibility. As he sailed into this inland sea he noted the very high mountains to the South East of the sea and turned North as this might lead to the "Passage" believed to exist to Hudson's Bay. As he explored North East into this Sea he went around an island in the middle and noted the latitude and longitude as well as noting the positions of several mountain peaks on top of the mountain ranges to the East and West of this Sea. He even noted that one of the prominent mountains to the East was defiantly volcanic.

What amazed my father was that the latitude and longitude Bartolome gave for the island he found could only be one place, The Marysville/ Sutter Buttes just North of Yuba City located in the Sacramento Valley!! The Volcanic mountain he located to the East matches Mount Lassen and the other high peak to the West matches Goose Mountain.

How is it that HE was Sailing around the Sacramento Valley in 1543? The account further described that after considerable exploration he realized that the water level was going down. When the tops of submerged trees began to appear he realized that this was some sort of flood and quickly headed back to the ocean. While the accounts are fragmentary as some of the records were later lost overboard in a terrible storm and replaced by memory, the account gives us some incredibly valuable information.

The explorer who is given credit for finding San Francisco Bay is Gaspar de Portola, it wasn't until November 4th 1769. After Bartolome Ferrelo returned in 1543/ 1544 the Spanish didn't send any more expeditions up the California coast until 1765.

Spain was not interested in this Northern coast until after Miguel Lopez de Legazpi completed the conquest of the Philippine Islands in 1565. With a Spanish Colony in the Philippines they were able to access trade goods from China and Japan. Originally they tried to return to South America with their trade ships but the Japanese current and a storm caught one of these ships and took it to Point Reyes California, where it was ship-wrecked. The crew managed to build a small open boat from the wreckage and local timber and with amazing luck and perseverance sailed all the way from Point Reyes to the Southern Mexican Mainland.

The speed of this Northern crossing and the fear of a Russian invasion in the 1700's was what prompted these later explorations up the Northern coast.

So while the credit of discovery for San Francisco Bay has been given to Gaspar de Portola in 1769; the Maidu legend of a raft from God sailing around the Marysville Buttes during the great flood verifies that the first European to sail into San Franciso Bay was actually Bartolome Ferrelo in 1543. From Bartolome Ferrelo's account we can get a measure of the magnitude of this flood.

First we know by both his account and the Maidu story that he sailed around the Marysville Buttes, this means that the site of present day Marysville and Yuba City had to have been under water. Second, we know that Bartolome did not see the tops of the submerged trees for some time during his exploration. And last and Third, we know that Bartolome's ships were ocean going sailing ships. These required a much deeper draft than that of a typical river craft. Even if the 200 ton flagship San Salvador had stayed in San Francisco Bay he wouldn't have used the San Miguel because it was rigged with lateen sails which offer poor maneuverability. While the San Miguel was equipped with slots for oars these were used to maneuver around a dock or for short distances. The crews had already been heavily reduced from a combination of scurvy and conflicts with Native Americans. By this time they were few in number and in too poor of a condition to use the oars, this leaves the La Victoria at 100 tons as the most likely vessel used.

From my experience as a Petty Officer Second Class in the US Navy and personnel experiences with sailing, boating and operating a barge, it is my opinion that Bartolome Ferrelo would have been taking soundings (finding the depth of the water by lowering a measuring rope with a weight on the end) as he progressed up this inland sea. While the documents my father had did not have sounding charts, it is almost certain that he was taking them. After consulting the instructors at the Wooden Boat Foundation in Port Townsend Washington, I got some particulars for the sailing ships of this period.

JUAN RODRIGUEZ CABRILLO.

João Rodrigues Cabrilho

Since the La Victoria was a 100 ton sea going sailing ship it would probably be about 16 feet wide and have at least a six foot draft and be around 60 feet long as calculated by Naval Architect Tim Nolan. This is if the cargo weight was 100 tons, however if this was the ship's weight then she would have been much bigger and deeper.

Next I have experience with the area in question, Yuba City and Marysville. In conferring with local tree services and the telephone company pole service employees, I have come up with about 100 feet as the maximum height for most Valley White Oaks and Cottonwood trees in that area.

Finally I have the San Francisco sectional aeronautical chart. This gives the topographical features for both the Sacramento and San Joaquin Valleys with their variations in altitude.

If we take it that Bartolome Ferrelo must have sailed over Yuba City which, is at 58 feet above sea level, in a ship with a 6 foot deep rudder, he also must have cleared the tops of submerged trees that often get to be 100 feet or more tall. This sets the water level of this inland sea at least 180 to possibly 200 feet above sea level. While Ferrelo could have sailed in water only 10 feet deep with the La Victoria, had it been that shallow he would have seen the trees and brush sticking out above the water and seen the event for the flood it was much earlier in his exploration. We also have the Maidu observation that it took nine days after he sailed back before they saw the waters go down. This would indicate that Ferrelo saw the tree tops appear and left but it was nine more days before the water had gone down enough to expose the land.

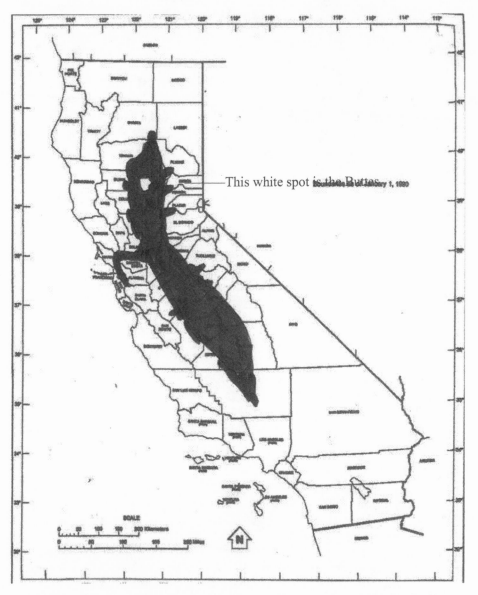

This white spot is the Buttes.

From my calculations and topographic maps this is the approximate size of the "inland sea" explored by

Using the data from the Sutter-by-pass it would seem that the water was closer to 100 plus feet deep in the Yuba City area to account for these observations. The Sutter Butte summit of 2140 feet would for example have been an island over one thousand nine hundred feet above this inland sea's level.

The state capitol of Sacramento could have been under 160 feet of water. Chico to the North and Merced to the South would also have been under water. This inland sea would have been about 250 miles North to South and probably 80 miles wide East to West.

As Bartolome Ferrelo did not venture South we don't know the extent of this flood to the South. We don't know how much the prior snow storms had hit the Southern Sierra Nevada, or if the warm heavy rain storm had been wide enough to have included the Southern Sierra Nevada. With this in mind the inland sea could have gone all the way to Bakersfield in the South if the storm had been wide enough.

Even with the minimum possible size that could account for these facts, the disruption this flood would have caused the Native peoples of California would have been enormous. If as the Maidu story says they used to live on the valley floor, then this flood would have destroyed all their supplies of stored food. The Elk and deer would have been drowned in large numbers. The deer and Elk herds in the foothills and mountains would have been driven down to the valley floor by the earlier heavy snow only to be then drowned by the subsequent valley flood. While some deer and elk obviously survived they would have been few in number for many years and in very poor condition for months after this disaster.

The Maidu population probably suffered a loss of at least 75% of their people. The disaster followed by a famine and contaminated water sources (cholera), could have killed 80% to 90% of the population if we use other similar historic events.

The flood of 1543 reduced the human population by such a large degree that I believe it's effects were still being felt by the Native California population in 1776, when the first Missionaries began to observe them. The first missionaries in California noted that there was little warfare amongst the Native Tribes and that their populations were fairly low and dispersed. In the 235 years from the flood to the missionaries observations there were probably eleven generations (assuming 20 years to the generation more or less). It was more than likely that the Native population had only recently recovered and as such had not yet been driven to large scale tribal warfare. If the flood of 1543 had not happened or if the Spanish had explored California in say 1520 they might have had a very different set of observations about the native populations.

In my Fathers report he concluded that there are no structures that can be made by man that would prevent a full flooding disaster in the Sacramento and San Joaquin Valleys, if an event like 1543 were to occur. His advice that in order to avoid the disaster of a 1543 scale event, would be to have all large population centers located on ground at or above 200 feet in elevation. The Maidu came to that same conclusion.

Native technologies

With no available deposits of copper or iron, these people went in different directions in their research. In biochemical research they made some incredible achievements that we are only now beginning to realize the scope of.

One such technology was only recently discovered. With an archeological record dating back more than 4,000 years we have examples of atlatal points using

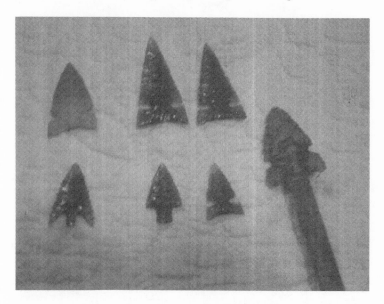

Clovis technology. Later, we see arrowheads and knives done to exacting detail using the Silurian pressure-flaking technique. About 1,400 years ago the arrowheads suddenly got very small. These were scoffed-at as being some sort of "bird point", however, these small arrow heads were found in the bones of elk and grizzly bear.

To most scientists as well as modern hunters this seemed very strange. You see, the way an arrow kills an animal is by causing a large internal hemorrhage. The ideal shot is to place an arrow just behind the front shoulder-bone of an animal, with the head of the arrow going through one side of the rib cage but not into the opposing side, penetrating the animal's lungs and the arteries coming out of the top of the heart. The action of the animal's leg moving shifts the shoulder bone back and forth, in a sideways direction, causing the arrows head to cut the lungs to pieces resulting in tremendous hemorrhaging and a quick death.

For all other areas of this continent as well as Europe, Africa and Asia, this requires an arrow head about three quarters of an inch wide and about two inches long. The "bird points" were usually less than half an inch wide by one inch long. We have examples in museums of the actual bows and arrows. The bows were strange as well. For all other areas, the bow usually had a draw weight (casting force) of forty pounds or more. These bows had draw weights usually less than thirty pounds with some as little as twenty five pounds. My ancestral Osage tribe had bows with draw weights of seventy to ninety pounds. That these California tribes were using such tiny arrow heads and weak bows on the very largest and most dangerous animals on earth was very puzzling. (Note, the California Grizzly Bear was actually larger than the Alaskan Kodiak Bear).

This mystery was solved in 1995 when a researcher discovered there was a residue on the bird point arrows in their collection, this residue was found to be a neurotoxin. This neurotoxin was apparently derived from one of the Cellar spiders we collectively call Daddy Long Legs. We don't know how they extracted or refined this neurotoxin, but as enzyme based toxins degrade in a mater of hours, we are very curious to find out how they stabilized this enzyme based neurotoxin.

The technology employed by these people was to have a cane arrow shaft with fletching (feather vanes) that was separate, from the fore-shafts which were kept in a small pouch hung about the neck. There were a number of these bird points attached to small shafts that stuck out of the top of the pouch.

The Maidu or Miwok hunter would reach into the top of the pouch and grasp the end of the wooden shaft. He would then take it out and mount it into the front end of the cane arrow shaft. Then with his very low powered bow he would target the animals rump (or really any place) and get the point of the arrow under the skin into the flesh. The idea was to not scare the animal, but only inflict a wound comparable to a scratch they might get from a dead limb or blackberry bush.

The feathered shaft would then fall off to be picked up by the hunter to use again. The neurotoxin laden bird-point, with its small wooden shaft, remained in the animal. From estimates of the residue they believe the animal would have gone into total paralysis in as little as one to seven minutes. This would indeed be a good tool for bringing down the largest and the most dangerous animals in North America.

We don't know how the Maidu extracted the venom, or how or with what they preserved the venom. We only know that they did. Considering that this technology survived the great flood, it is interesting to wonder what other biochemical achievements these people made.

The primary starch in these peoples' diet came from acorn meal. The process of leaching out the tannic acid and grinding the meal into a form suitable for cooking was a science. The very type of stone used for grinding was particularly important. For example the Maidu had discovered long ago not to use Serpentine for their mortars as the metals in it would cause stomach ulcers.

Europeans could have avoided the problems with asbestos if they had consulted the Native California population.

Another technology they had was a form of telegraph system for rapid communication, called "Singing Stones". These bedrock formations are for that

Pictured to the left are several replicas of Maidu tools. On the far left is an Atlatal head, this was made when Clovis technology was the state-of-the-art and denotes the period 3,000 or more years ago. An Atlatal point like this was found in a Volkswagen-sized armadillo shell in a cave near Cool.

The two knives to the right are made by pressure flaking and are the state of the art in stone tools.

Below are a set of pictures of the author with a deer taken with stone tools. The obsidian knife in the center was used to gut, skin and debone the deer.

This deer was taken using a traditional Osage sinew backed bow with flint arrowheads on cedar shafts with left wing turkey feather fletching. The two arrows went into the deer approximately eight inches and one was broken off when the deer fell.

The buck went about twenty five yards before falling from the two arrows. The stone age tools were very effective.

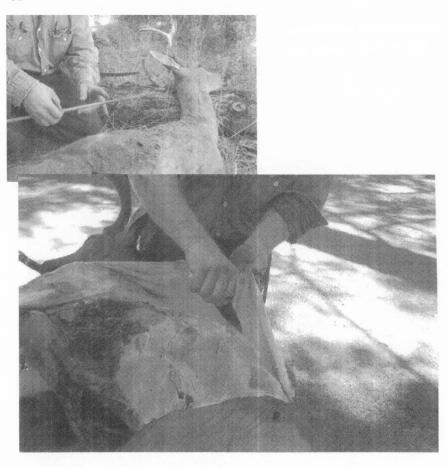

The stone knife was very sharp and did not dull or lose it's edge in the entire project.

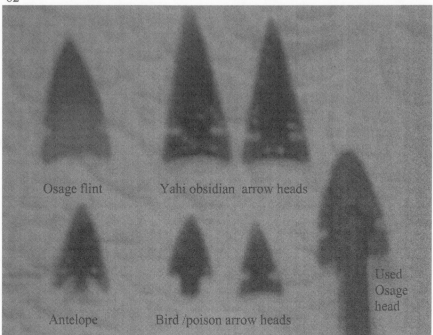

Osage flint   Yahi obsidian arrow heads

Antelope   Bird /poison arrow heads   Used Osage head

The replica arrowheads to the left are, from left-to-right top row, an Osage flint Missouri, then two Yahi Obsidieon arrowheads from Lassen County California. Bottom-row left is a Shoshone antelope point from Modoc County. Then two bird-points (poison arrows) as used by the Maidu and Miwok in Northern California; and last, the flint Osage arrowhead recovered from the Blacktail deer taken by the author. The Neuro-toxin enabled these people to use very a different hunting strategy.

Both animals were photographed by the author in the immediate area of No-Po-Chitta Toma and Hekeke-Toma. Their ancestors were the food and fear of the Maidu residents of No-Po-Chitta Toma, as are these individuals to today's human residents.

Pictured above are two very different animals as far as killing them with a stone arrowhead. The deer has a thin hide and the vital area is often exposed; while the bear is very heavily muscled with a thick hide. Maidu/ Miwok neuro-toxin technology rendered them equal to take.

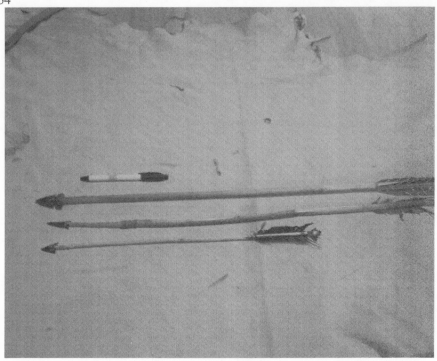

Pictured above; an Osage arrow, below it is an example of a Maidu poison arrow with the detachable arrowhead insert, and on the bottom is an example of the small Maidu poison arrow. Both of the Maidu arrows used the Neuro toxin and there fore had the unique small "Bird" point.

Pictured below to the left is a close up of the detachable "Bird" point equipped Maidu arrow.

Pictured below to the right is a comparison close up of the Osage point (just below the ink pen) and beneath it the detachable "Bird" point Maidu arrow.

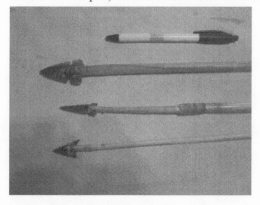

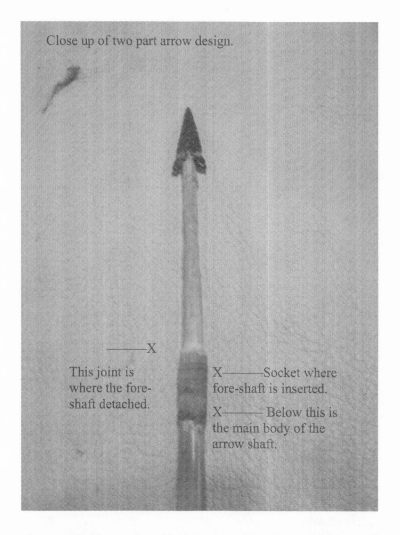

Close up of two part arrow design.

————X
This joint is
where the fore-
shaft detached.

X————Socket where
fore-shaft is inserted.

X———— Below this is
the main body of the
arrow shaft.

In contrast, the poison tree frogs of South America used for their neurotoxin by many tribes including the Yanomano for their blow gun darts, require that the poison must be freshly derived from the frogs to maintain maximum potency. This necessitates that a supply of these frogs be kept on hand. The California tribes on the other hand, using the Cellar Spiders neurotoxin, found a way to stabilize it so that an arrow over one hundred years old still has a lethal potency.

This process, lost to history, is the focus of considerable research by today's toxicologists. These California Natives developed this process and used it for thousands of years, yet modern day man cannot figure out how they did this.

MAIDU TERRITORY

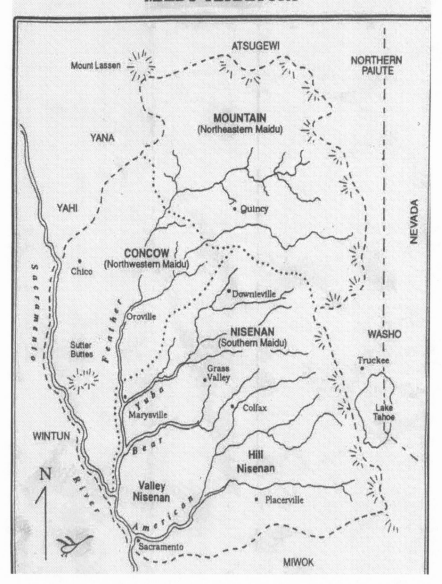

The original border between the Miwok and Maidu is the broken line pictured at the bottom of this map. Even before 1848 slave raids by the Miwok had forced the Maidu to pull back to the North side of the South Fork of the American River. This was after the loss of an estimated 500 people and the abandoning of three major Maidu villages.

surface where a person can tap on a face (end grain) of the stone and another person can clearly hear the taps at another point of the bedrock surfacing sometimes fifteen or more miles away.

"Telegraph operators" would be stationed at these "Singing Stones" with runners available to take messages to the villages or relay stations. This concept is not mysterious. The children's toy telephone constructed with two empty cans and a string connecting the bottom of both cans, works on the same principal. With the string pulled taut one child can talk into his can while the other child hears them by listening in the other can. The same is done when a person puts their ear on a railroad track and can hear an approaching train over an hour before it arrives. The bedrock in the Sierra Nevada foothills and mountains frequently has long stretches in it that are not fractured. By accessing two opposing ends of such a structure one can clearly hear taps generated on the other end.

Most of these "Singing Stones" lines run in the same direction as the uplifted rock formations. In the Sierra Nevada this is generally Southwest to Northeast. There are some shorter formations that have been compressed and two ends of the formation are exposed across a valley in a sort of U shape. This enables information to be transmitted in an East to West direction.

Unfortunately the Europeans thought the listening stations of these "Singing Stones" were some sort of pagan altars. They often shot at the Indians and also tried to blow up the stones, thinking they were altars to pagan gods. It would have been fascinating to talk to the Maidu and known where all these lines were, instead of blowing up the "telephone system".

They had a complete and rather nice religion with festivals throughout the year. The year was broken down into the four seasons; Spring: Yo-meni , Flowers; Summer: Kaukati, dust; Autumn: Se-meni, seeds; Winter: Ko-meni, Snow. The Hoktom in the spring, followed by the "Ilakum" in the dry season, usually in July. Then they had a "Ushtimo"or burning anniversary in September and then the "Yakai" near Christmas time. The primary festivals were in the springtime (Yo-meni), such as the Bear Dance (Weda). For the Weda the Maidu made large preparations. The date was established by the appearance of certain migratory birds and the start of certain frogs taking voice, the date was then set with knotted strings representing the number of days until the Bear Dance. These knotted strings were then sent out to smaller villages. For Garden Valley the Bear Dances were held in either Chicken Flat (Hekeke-Toma) or Moon Flat (No-po-Chitta-Toma), known by us as Columbia Flat.

The women wove special baskets (Bat-Ky) with symbols significant to the Bear Dance. Everyone dressed up with the girls having flowers in their hair and the men making new colorful headbands.

When all the people had arrived the festival started, with principal Chief Captain Juan (and later Coppa Hembo) giving an opening prayer thanking the Creator for getting them through the Winter and giving thanks for everyone who was able to come.

Then they started dancing, singing and gambling, there were special dances for specific purposes. A person could at this time of the year say the word Sola (Rattlesnake) . It was believed that if a person said the word Rattlesnake at other times of the year it would provoke the rattlesnakes to hunt that person and bite them. By about the fourth day of the festival the elders as well as children would go to the creek with special flower decorations. They would sing a song, "Snake, snake don't bite me.", then throw their decorations into the creek. This would appease the Snake-eater Man, a legendary bad man, so that he would not bother them for the rest of the year. The elders also spoke to the Bear spirit (the most powerful of all the spirits) to protect them and not to hurt them. (I saw this spirit once, very fascinating to me, in fact it helped my youngest son Jacob, who was a newborn in difficulty at that time.)

A Maidu story told to me went something like this; "Back in the time just after creation all the folks were animals and they were all biting and fighting each other. The Creator decided that this was enough and he called for everybody to come out and he was going to set out some rules and everybody was going to quit biting and fighting one another. Everybody came out and the Creator got to setting everybody up as to what they were to do and how they were supposed to act. Little grey fox (Joskopim) noticed that bear and rattlesnake weren't there. Molloko the vulture was closest to the sky and he went up high to look for bear and rattlesnake. Molloko saw bear (Pano) sneaking across the Valley (Kojo) to get into the brush in the mountain (Yamanim). The Creator and Little Grey fox (Joskopim) went over to the mountain (Yamanim) where Porcupine (Ch onim yamanim) told the Creator that he had heard the Rattle (Csa-can-tay) over under the rock there. The Creator moved the rock and Rattlesnake (sola) tried to slither away but the Creator stepped on his head squashing it flat. Just then bear (Pano) jumped out of a bush nearby and made a run for it. The Creator grabbed the end of Pano's tail but Pano was struggling so hard that the end of Pano's tail came off in the creators hand. This caused the Creator to fall back and lose his footing on Rattlesnake (sola) who slithered under an even bigger rock. That is why bear (Pano) has such a short tail and why rattlesnakes (sola) head is flat and why them two still try to bite you."

In the Bear Dance (Weda) one person was chosen to wear a bearskin and act like a bear. The bear actor would claw the ground and act the way a bear does when they are searching for food. People played four hole flutes made from elder berry vines and beat small drums. Children would be allowed to go into the circle and chase the bear with little switches while the older people said prayers, then other people would come in and dance with the bear actor. In the end the Chief, carrying a pole on which were tied the white feathers of a snow goose, followed the bear actor to a creek where the bear actor was able to wash. By the 1890's during the last of these Bear Dances, (when Coppa Hembo was Chief), the Maidu would fire guns in the air.

A local Black Bear (Pano in Maidu) from Spanish Flat named Skipper who more than lived up to the old Maidu story.

Maidu Controlled the Land

The early settlers looked out on the landscape and saw a virgin wilderness, in reality it was rather manicured. The Maidu cultivated their lands in ways we are only now realizing. Today we see thick stands of manzanita in the two to four thousand foot elevations and impenetrable thickets of creosote brush from two thousand feet all the way to sea level.

The Maidu and natural fire never allowed these species to get so large. By using fire in the fall, these seed sprouting brush species were heavily reduced while the stump sprouting species (particularly the varieties of Ceonothus Lemoni "deer brush") were fertilized and encouraged.

Even the color of the landscape has changed. Gold Hill which stands above the Coloma Gold Discovery site, was not a golden color fifty years before gold was discovered there. The native bunch grass species stayed

Only recently have we learned that the Maidu were correct in how to manage a forest using controlled fire.

green year round but introduced Mediterranean grass species from the missions had reached the Maidu country only fifty years before the gold rush. These bunch grass species had a hard time competing with the new species but remained a large percentage of the coverage until heavy grazing, particularly by sheep, decimated them to their now-trace-levels. The Mediterranean grass species did several other things; the large, majestic White Oak trees you see in the central valley and foothills could no longer reproduce because the new grass choked out their seedlings. To see the effect note that you do not see any young White Oaks. The species is nearly dead as most individuals are beyond their fertile age. Note, along I-5 from Sacramento to Redding and beyond, approximately 250 miles, the magnificent white oaks have no young. Efforts are being made to get some new youngsters started but interest and funds are severely short for such a massive project. These

Gold Hill today as it looks over Coloma.

The White Oak are dying from Mediterranean grasses.

forests are in greater danger than the tropical Rain Forests everyone is concerned about.

The new grass species began to invade and compete with species cultivated by the Maidu for centuries, the effects of the new grass species weren't completely negative, the California Quail numbers exploded on this new feed. Today there are arguments about the introduction of wild turkeys to these lands in that they are adversely affecting the landscape by competing with other indigenous species. In point of fact nearly everything has already been altered and few native species remain.

The records show that a typical family of two adults and four children would gather some 33,500 pounds of acorns in a two week period. The Maidu were known to be prepared for a "Rainy Day" or a bad acorn crop by having a three year or more supply of stored acorns.

Acorns gave the Maidu starch and fats but other foods, such as pine nuts, added protein. The "Digger Pine" so named because California natives were often seen digging under these trees gathering pine nuts. This pine species has recently had its name changed to Grey Pine in an attempt to be politically correct. Found at higher elevations the Sugar Pine nuts are delicious as well.

Other important plant species included the Indian Soap weed. The shucks around the onion-like bulb made fiber that was used to make mats and skirts. The bulb (properly leached) could be cooked and eaten much like an onion. The leaching, if done in large quantities, would drug the fish in a shallow pool of a creek, enabling the Maidu to grab up the fish while processing the Indian soap weed for consumption.

The native potato (about the size of a peanut) called (So Ko Mi) were

gathered and boiled. Manzanita berries were ground into flour and made bread.

The Spanish Moss we see hanging out of White Oaks in moist basins (A symbiotic algae and fungus combination) was used for baby diapers and toilet paper.

For protein they hunted Blacktail

Deer, Black Bear, Grizzly Bear, and Tule Elk. California Valley Quail were taken with bows and special arrows, as well as with low fences that herded the quail into funnels where nooses were set. Waterfowl were taken with special archery gear. Jackrabbits were

Guttenburgers Corner in Pleasant Valley today

taken by herding them into corrals/ fences where they were taken with special clubs similar to the Australian boomerang

The jackrabbits skins were cut into long strips that were cross woven and knotted to make blankets and shawls.

By 1849 the Maidu had 74 primary villages and numerous smaller camps. They had already lost at least four major villages to Miwok slave raids. These lost villages were located within a range of fifteen miles South of the South Fork of the American River. One large village was located South of the intersection of Pleasant Valley Road and Bucks Bar Road (Guttenburgers Corner).

Another was located in Happy Valley at the fork in the road leading to Grizzly Flats. Another was located on the Northwest side of the intersection of Pleasant Valley Road and Highway 49 in the Town of Diamond Springs

(the location of the three gas stations), the last major village was located just North of the present town of El Dorado called Onchoma.

These slave raids had reduced the Maidu population of El Dorado County by possibly five hundred or more persons by 1849. This loss of people had resulted in the Maidu tribe abandoning many of their Southern

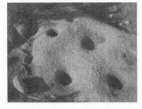

villages.

The Washoe Tribe

The Washoe inhabited the High Sierra in summer with Lake Tahoe being vital to their culture and food supply.

Maidu Chiefs with American Peace Commissioners in 1851.

The Maidu Village of (Banak am Mo-luk) was located across the street to the right of the sign here in Diamond Springs at Hwy 49 and Pleasant Valley Road.

Due to deep snows they wintered in the Carson Valley, Honey lake and the West slope into Pleasant Valley and Garden Valley.

The Washoe were estimated to number approximately 1,500 or more in the 1700's. By 1845 they had been reduced to approximately 1,000 members due to Northern Piute slave raids. The Washoe captives were sold to the New Mexicans and Mexicans in trade for horses.

A Washoe family living along lake Tahoe pictured in 1898 along the South Shore. The Lady of the Lake is a sacred site of the Washoe.

The Washoe winter areas in the Carson Valley had by the late 1830's be-come dangerous as the Piute slavers mounted on horseback had all the advan-tages to run them down and grab them. The Washoe were now forced to live higher in the mountains where thicker cover, rocks and boulders denied the horse mounted Piute the advantage. The heart of the Washoe winter range was (by 1840) the area of present day Markleeville California.

The Washoe had been an important trader with the Miwok and Maidu for nearly 3,000 years. They exported prime pieces of obsidian from the volcanic cinder cones on the East side of the Sierra Nevada, trading for salmon, acorn meal and sea shells as well as other goods.

One of their major trails was the present day Highway 88 and Mormon Emi-grant Trail otherwise known as Iron Mountain Road. This trail was utilized by Kit Carson and now the pass is known as Carson Pass and Carson Spur. For thousands of years the Washoe used this trail to transport obsidian. The Washoe did not have to take their goods all the way to the villages of the Maidu and Miwok but established a "trading center" roughly at the intersection of Mormon Emigrant Trail/ Iron Mountain Road and North South Road, here the other tribes brought their goods to meet the Washoe and do business.

The arrival of the Spanish ended this several thousand year old trade as the Miwok were now getting steel knives and other goods, including horses, in exchange for slaves. With the Maidu losing Pleasant Valley to the Miwok the Washoe were walking right into slavers if they continued down the ancient trail. Many Washoe were using the Rubicon Trail from Lake Tahoe to Wentworth Springs to get access to the Maidu on the Georgetown Divide. The Maidu did not have access to the Spanish iron goods and still needed obsidian.

The Lady of The Lake at Lake Tahoe in Nevada a ceremonial site of the Washoe People

The Maidu provided a refugee camp of sorts for the Washoe along Traverse

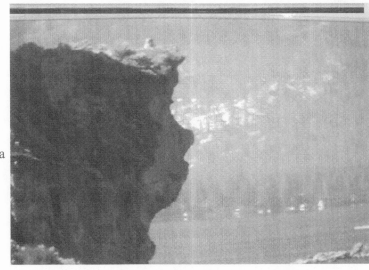

Creek, with one of the larger refugee villages being located South of the intersection of Meadow Brook Road and Bear Creek Road in the Serpentine formation there.

It was one of these refugee Washoe women who would marry a Maidu Man. Their son would be the last Chief of the Maidu tribe on the Georgetown Divide, Coppa Hembo.

This refuge for the Washoe was one of very few. The rest of the Washoe were conquered by the Northern Piute in 1860 and forbidden to have horses.

Pictured above is a small water fall coming down the nearly vertical stone face into the American River Canyon.

Below is one of the few open hillsides on the North side of the American River Canyon where the topography is often at the maximum angle of repose.

The primary source of carbohydrates for the Washoe were pinyon pine nuts and to a lesser degree acorns. The discovery of silver in Nevada's Comstock lode required fuel to operate their steam engines. The stands of pinyon pine, as well as any thing else in the area, was rapidly cut for fuel.

The loss of these resources, reduced fishing and the reduction in deer numbers forced the Washoe into closer contact with the whites. The Washoe wintering in the Honey lake area were reduced to starvation by the grazing of sheep on their lands. These starving Washoe tried to pick potatoes from the settlers farms in the Honey lake area. This became known as the "Potato War of 1857".

Of the approximately 1,000 Washoe left in 1845, only 500 were left by 1866. Most of these few were in the Markleville area and the Georgetown Divide, with a few living off the pancakes of a nice white settler named Joseph Grey. Grey had built a cabin on the shore of the Lake Tahoe and enjoyed the company of the Washoe.

The group of Washoe living around Joseph Grey on the shore of Lake Tahoe were vital to the other remaining Washoe. They were near the "Lady of the Lake" also known as Cave Rock on the East side of lake. This was one of the most sacred sites of the Washoe people and was used for many observances as well as burials.

The Washoe tried in every way to make friends of the newly arrived Americans. The Americans could provide protection from Piute slavers and by working on American owned farms and ranches in the Carson Valley they wouldn't be removed from their ancestral homelands to reservations. Many intermarried with other tribes and white ranchers as well as a large population who became farm laborers for the Carson Valley grain farms.

It wasn't until the 1990's that the number of people who descend from Washoe finally recovered to pre 1849 levels.

The Rise of the Paiute.

The Northern Paiute had lived in Northern Nevada, Southern Idaho, the Northeast part of California and Southeast part of Oregon. They were related to the Ute tribe of Utah but their name was interpreted as "Water Ute" or "True Ute" giving them their prefix.

For centuries they had made a living from gathering Pinyon Pine nuts. They cultivated several grass species along Walker Lake's delta to produce a sort of barley. The tubers of the lake tule plants were cultivated and several insect species larvae were harvested in season. They hunted the antelope and Mule deer as well as jackrabbit and waterfowl.

They had been one of the primary victims of Modoc slave raids for centuries. Then in the early 1800's they began to acquire horses. The horse transformed the Paiute, with the horse they could master the resources of their desert environment. This resulted in an increase in their population, it also made them eager to get more horses. The primary sources were the Mew Mexican ranchos and Mexicans in the states of Sonora and Chihuahua, who were more than willing to trade slaves for horses. This trade would continue well after the American Civil War, as the Mexicans were still buying slaves from the North well into the 1890's.

The Great Basin through which many of the 49er's came was by that time severely depopulated. Those bands and tribes who were more sedentary, or tied to agriculture, had been easy prey and were all but absent by that time.

The Paiute now with horses, even tried to take slaves from the West side of the Sierra Nevada. A slave raiding party of Paiute Led by Chief Pico had come all the way to the present day location of Cool California. They were after slaves but came across a white man named Avery and killed him for his horse and gun.

The local Maidu helped an El Dorado sheriff named E.L. Parker run down these Paiute who were over 150 miles from their tribal territory. The Maidu were more than helpful to the Americans in ridding their lands of this menace.

The horse gave the Northern Paiute a tremendous advantage over the Modoc and by the late 1850's the two tribes were having almost constant battles, until the end of the Modoc War in 1873. I will go into that conflict in detail in a later chapter dealing with the Paiute, Modoc and Klamath tribes.

The horse was not necessarily an advantage to the Maidu, Miwok or Washoe living in the foothills and mountains of California for two reasons. First; prior to irrigation there were few natural meadows with green grass year-round available for horse feed. Second; the steep brushy terrain limited where a horse could travel. Note that the Maidu helping Sheriff Parker were on foot and still caught up with the Horse mounted Paiute near Cool.

The Battle of Rock Creek was between a Miwok force who had crossed into Maidu territory and the Maidu plus a few of their Washoe allies.

The battleground was in the Rock Creek Drainage, approximately one

The open ridge descending from the South Rim of the American River Canyon where the Maidu observers first saw the approaching Miwok Army as they came down to the ford in the river. By using singing stones and runners they were able to quickly mobilize a response army of Miadu and Washoe who caught the Miwok force in Rock Creek Canyon and defeated them in 1848.

half mile upstream from the confluence of Rock Creek into the American River. Located just below and to the West of Swansbrough/ Mosquito (Sy-hy-lim-Toma), and to the East of Spanish Flat, Barley Flat and Columbia Flat (Po-No-Chitta Toma).

The Battle occurred in the late Fall (Se-meni) of 1848. The American River was at it's lowest level making the Maidu homeland more vulnerable to slave raids as the women and children were out gathering acorns.

Maidu sentries first observed the Miwok forces coming down the open white oak covered ridge that terminates on the opposite side of the American River from the confluence of Rock Creek. The Maidu sentry perched on

The Battle of Rock Creek (Wokitto-oosew)

The American River Canyon at this point was the border between the Maidu lands, with rolling table country located on top of the Georgetown Divide to the North and the Miwok country to the South. Here, near the confluence with Rock Creek, the canyon walls are nearly vertical above a roaring chasm of white water. The small streams coming off the Divide from the North fall down inaccessible vertical stone faces. The only ford in the American River and topographical access into and out of the river is at the confluence with Rock Creek.

The topography of the land determined the place of battle. While comparatively small this bloody battle is representative of a great many conflicts and carnage that never made it into current history books.

Fought with poisoned arrows, clubs, axes and bare hands this battle was observed and monitored from Castle Rock, where a "Singing Stone" linked this post with the villages of No-po-chitta-Toma, Syhylim-Toma and three other villages in the area. The speed of communications enabled a force, large enough to counter and defeat the invasion to be quickly assembled.

Castle Rock gave the alarm and two braves were dispatched to screen the Miwoks movements until Maidu and Washoe forces could be assembled.

By using "Singing Stones" and a signal fire probably located on Slate Mountain, along the same formation (ridge) near where Ray Little's family's gold mine is now located, they put out the alarm and location of the attacking force.

Maidu warriors assembled from Chicken Flats (Hekeke-Toma), Barley Flats, Columbia Flat (Po-no-Chitta-Toma) and a small village located on Darling Ridge on the South end of the present day "Old Eells Place". The Maidu and Washoe were under the combined leadership of Coppa Hembo and Captain Juan, with several of his sons including his oldest, who was killed in this battle.

The Washoe Warriors coming from their refugee camp along Traverse Creek also arrived in time to help the Maidu in this battle. The Maidu and Wash forces converged on the area from two trails. The main force combined on the ridge below Barley Flats and took the lower end of the One Eye Trail to the ridge below Castle Rock. The other force coming down from Darling Ridge (Old Ells Place) had already arrived and was shadowing the Miwa. The two Maidu warriors who had been screening the movements of the advancing Miwa called to the main force of Maidu, who now descended into the Rock Creek Canyon, ma-

Pictured above the Maidu observation post on Castle Rock, part of the Talking Stone network, used during the Battle of Rock Creek.

neuvering to get a favorable position to use their poison arrows from above.

Readers should realize that even a scratch from these poison arrows could be lethal.

The confluence of Rock Creek and the American River (The Ford)

Chief Coppa Hembo the last chief of the Maidu living in
Mosquito (Sy-hy-lim), Chicken Flats (Hekeke-Toma), Garden Valley and Irish Creek. Story has it that his mother
was Washoe and his father Maidu.

The attacking force of Miwok were led by a warrior wearing a cotton shirt with large vertical red stripes and a straw hat with a strip of cloth sewn along the brim. As the two forces closed in, both sides were shouting at one another. Several arrows were discharged but either the range was too long or there were some canyon winds and they fell short. One of the Maidu warriors from Darling Ridge had a steel axe while several of the Miwa possessed steel axes. Otherwise all the weapons were stone age.

It had taken the Miwa longer to cross the American River than they had wished and the Maidu had arrived before they could climb out of the canyon. The fight was close, as the steep sides of Rock Creek Canyon confined them and limited their ability to maneuver.

The actual Battle occurred along Rock Creek just upstream of its confluence with Mosquito Creek (Shyly Semi). A major Maidu trail connecting the villages at Mosquito (Sy-hy-lim) (Swansborough) with the villages from Darling Ridge to Garden Valley (Chicken Flat (Hekeke-Toma) and Columbia Flat) Po-no-Chitta-Toma.

The trail going down from Mosquito (Syhylim-Toma), along Mosquito Creek to Chicken Flats, (Hekeke-Toma) was where, years before, Coppa Hembo and two companions had been attacked by a Grizzly Bear. While both of his friends tried to run, Coppa Hembo drew his bow and managed to get two poisoned arrows into the Grizzly before the bear struck him in the head knocking him to the ground. Coppa raised himself and managed to get one more arrow into the bear before passing out. Coppa lay unconscious, and from a distance, his friends believed he was dead but the bear was still thrashing so they left.

Coppa Hembo came-to and skinned the now-dead Grizzly. The scar on Coppa's head from the Grizzly's blow would be visible for the rest of his life.

Coppa eventually came into the Village at Mosquito (Syhylim-Toma) carrying the Bears skin. He was then given the name "Coppa Hembo" which means Bear Killer in Maidu.

A local Black Bear (Pano) in Maidu

Now in the Battle of Rock Creek, Coppa Hembo and the other Maidu and Washoe were fighting the Miwok to save their people from slavery. Chief Captain Juan's oldest son and several others drew into hand to hand combat killing several Miwok, but Captain Juan's son was mortally wounded. His name has been lost because Maidu tradition does not speak the name of the dead. A score or so of Maidu were killed or wounded, but the majority of the dead were Miwok. The Miwok now had to make a retreat back down Rock Creek and across the American River while being attacked by the Maidu, who inflicted several more casualties, thus ended the Battle of Wokitto-oosew.

Coppa Hembo and the majority of Maidu and Washoe warriors carried the dead back to their villages, the others operated as a screening force against the retreating Miwok. It was near sundown on the following day when Coppa and the Maidu from Chicken Flats came in bringing in the body of the Chiefs son. Captain Juan and villagers of Chicken Flats (Hekeke-Toma) as well as Columbia Flat (Po-No-Chitta-Toma) and the Washoe Camp all came to the burial grounds along Irish Creek. The Chiefs son was burned and the "Cry" went on for more than a week.

The fall storms caused the river to rise and the border river became impassable ending the threat of Miwok raids.

In Coloma James Marshal's discovery of gold at Sutters Mill had by now caused a rush on the area. Most of John Sutter's work force had left him for the gold rush and were descending on the Maidu and Miwok areas in search

The Kelsey School House in Columbia Flat (No-Po-Chitta-Toma) Coloma today.

of gold.

In the group at Coloma was Caleb Greenwood with his sons and daughters and a group of Oregon fur trappers. There is a lot of misinformation about Caleb Greenwood. He had left Virginia as a young man and gone into the Rocky Mountains as a fur trapper. He did not marry until he was 63 years old and his wife, Batchicka Youngcault, was a Crow Indian woman. They had 5 sons and two daughters. His last daughter Mojave Greenwood was born when he was 80 years old. His wife Batchicka Greenwood, died shortly after the birth of Mojave as a result of complications from the delevery. In 1844 when Caleb Greenwoods oldest sons, John and Britt, were hired as guides to lead a wagon-train out to California, so Caleb "Old Man" Greenwood took his family to California. They were reported to have been at Sutter's Fort in 1846 when the Bear Flag was raised but Greenwood established his family around Clear Lake. Although he was 92 years old he was active and working, for example, he scouted the route for a wagon-trail (today's interstate 80) along the Carson River. After completing this job, he led another wagon trail from Colorado back to California before the year was out!

When Greenwood got word that the Donner Party was stranded he was in Yerba Buena, (now San Francisco), he rode the 70 miles to Clear Lake and then sent his second oldest son with food and supplies to the Donner Party 150 miles away. His son was friends with the Maidu and one of those Maidu (rumored to be Coppa Hembo) were the first to arrive at the Donner Party bringing supplies, an amazing feat of speed and endurance.

The Greenwoods were part of the Oregon Trappers. They were among the first to arrive at Coloma for the gold rush among them was a young John Steele.

It should be noted that Caleb Greenwood's daughters were the "Bells of Coloma" and were courted (and eventually) married by wealthy miners. The fact that they were half Indian was not a problem and they and their brothers were prominent businessmen and community leaders whose descendants are still leading citizens in Placerville and Sacramento.

In the winter (Ko-meni) of 1848, with the river level down due to the cold weather, a raiding party of Miwok crossed the American River into the Maidu country and came across an Oregon man in Kelsey Canyon down-stream of Chili Bar.

The Miwok in Placerville had been employed by Captain Charles Weber, he had been an agent of John Sutter and the Mexicans. They arrived with a group of Plains Miwok to look for gold.

Mr. Weber set up operations along Pull-Pull–Mull Creek and his Indian laborers began digging out gold, the creek would later be named for Charles Weber. In

Weber's camp were several Spanish and Mexican men and at least one
Englishman, they were telling the local Miwok to fear the Oregon Men.
There was legitimate reason for the Miwok to fear the Oregon Men but
behind this was the very-real fact that they were a threat to Weber's and
Sutter's operations.

The Miwok were more inclined to believe what Weber's men were telling
them because the Oregon men were allies of their enemies the Maidu, who
only a few months before had killed many of their warriors in the Battle of
Rock Creek.

The First Indian War of El Dorado County, 1849

It was in this state of desire for revenge that the Miwok raiding party

came across the Oregon man in Kelsey Canyon and killed him. On the

Webber Creek (Pul Pul Mull) in Maidu. Captain Charles Weber had
brought 25 Valley Miwok from near present day Stockton under Chief
Jose Jesus and set up eight miles down stream of here (Weber's Dig-
gings). Weber's Miwok were said to have recovered over 400 ounces of
Gold there in 1848 and 1849. These Miwok and some of Weber's associates encouraged (paid) the local Mountain Miwok to attack Oregon Men
who were a source of competition. This lead to a punitive raid by the Oregon Men Under the Command of John Greenwood and lead by Maidu
scouts to a Miwok Village (Wu Hu-Luk) located about 75 yards down

stream of this location (the crossing of Cedar Ravine Road with Weber Creek). In the battle thirty Miwok were killed and another thirty were taken (captive). Some of the Captives were Maidu who had been taken earlier by the Miwok for slaves. In Wu Hu-Luk one of the "Missing Oregon Men's rifle was found as well as new English and Spanish Coins indicating some of the Miwok had been paid to kill or run off Oregon Men.

ridge above were Maidu women and children from Columbia Flat (Po-No-Chitta-Toma) who were collecting acorns and saw the whole thing. They gave the alarm and Warriors from Columbia and Chicken Flat as well as several Oregon Men, arrived before the Miwok war party could kidnap any of the Maidu women and children. The Miwok re-crossed the American River, believing they would be safe from retaliation by the Maidu. The Oregon Men wanted to get the killers and the Maidu were eager to see their old enemies get a taste of the kind of fear they had endured for years. Once a suitable party of Oregon Men was ready, several Maidu from Columbia Flat led them to the Miwok village (In-Dak) across the American River just below present day Placerville.

Once there, the Oregon Men acted like law enforcement. Only the killers identified by the Maidu (who had witnessed the murder) were taken and justice was administered.

This event made some of Webers Miwok even more angry, with a little coaxing and liquor from Weber's associates they were ready to go again by February (Yo-meni) 1849. This was a "standard practice" for Mexican California. A gold discovery in 1798, just North of Los Angeles in Placerita Canyon, was kept secret until 1842 by beating or killing Indians who commented on seeing any gold. This was done by Priests and Dons alike. Placerita Canyon produced an estimated five million dollars, but it was kept by local Mexican authorities.

It should be noted that Weber's Miwok were actually a group of 25 Plaines Miwok led by Chief Jose Jesus. Captain Weber had brought them with him from near Stockton. These were not local Miwok but they and Webber's associates encouraged the local Miwok into violent acts that might benefit their interests.

Oregon Men were now on both sides of the American River, and were going all over Miwok lands as well. Two Oregon men were working the confluence of Martinez Creek and the North Fork of the Cosumnes River when Miwok killed them. A war-party of Miwok were believed to have been responsible for the killing of several Oregon men on Murderers Bar on the North Fork of the American River. Additionally several other Oregon Men suddenly disappeared, and the belief was that the Miwok were responsible.

Caleb Greenwood's sons John and David were elected to lead a party of

Kelsey Canyon where the Miwok slave-raiding party (after crossing the American River below Chili Bar) came across an Oregon man and killed him. This was observed by Maidu women and children from Chicken Flats, who were gathering acorns on the ridge to the right and gave the alarm. Having been discovered the Miwok party beat a retreat back across the American River.

Oregon men to retaliate against the Miwok killers, several Maidu warriors were more than willing to serve as guides. By early April 1849 the party of Oregon Men, under the command of John Greenwood departed from Coloma and headed for the Miwok Village along Webers Creek, (Pull-Pull– Mull) called Wu-Hu-luk. This was located just downstream of the present day crossing of Cedar Ravine Road, just South of Placerville. Wu-Hu-Luk Village was not Webber's band under Chief Jose Jesus but an indigenous village of Miwok numbering nearly 80 individuals.

In the attack, the Miwok Chief of Wu-Hu-Luk, was shot down three times as he continued to raise up repeatedly to fire arrows. Some 30 Miwok were killed and another 25 to 30 were taken captive. There are inconsistencies in the reports, as some of the "prisoners" were actually Maidu taken as slaves by the Miwok in earlier raids and were now able to return to their families.

One account said Greenwood and his men didn't find anything to connect these Miwok with the killings; while three accounts have them recovering one of the "Missing Oregon Men's" rifle in the village, these rifles were all hand made and as individual works could easily be identified. One account has it that this very rifle was later given to one of the Maidu scouts from Chicken Flats. This Maidu scout would make a living as a professional hunter with this rifle. His children would go to the school at Kelsey and become leading members of the Garden Valley community.

The party of Oregon Men returned to Coloma with the captured Indians and scalps, this shocked a visitor named Theodore T. Johnson. Johnson was taken aback by this event, not understanding this kind of battle.

In the group of prisoners were seven able bodied Miwok warriors. Nobody knew what should be done with them since there was no jail. The alternative of turning them loose would only mean they would probably be responsible for more murders.

It was probably decided that the seven warriors would get a chance to "run away", at which time five were killed, one was wounded, with the remaining warrior getting away. It should be realized that many of the Oregon Trappers were either married to Crow women or had Crow mothers and this was a common practice by the Crow for dealing with prisoners in a situation such as this.

The Placerville Militia also mustered out, led by Sheriff William Rogers. They killed only one Indian, of unknown origin who was probably unrelated to the events.

So ended the First Indian War of El Dorado County.

The Second Indian War of El Dorado County 1850 –1851

By the fall of 1849 Miwok raiding parties and confrontations with local Miwok were resulting in small battles all along the Western Slope of El Dorado County. Misinformation and fear on both sides, were compounded by a titanic rush of people from all over the world, descending in a crazed mass on the county. The men who had been the power brokers in the old Mexican land system (including many of John Sutters associates) were losing their grip on things and they didn't like it.

In this chaos some of the old liners were figuring out ways to make a profit. Several outfits operating near present day Rancho Murettia were offering Miwok warriors a good price for any slaves or livestock they could bring down to them. This arrangement for slaves had been long standing but now the cattle and horses of the American settlers and gold prospectors were fair game and could be fenced for a quick profit.

The site of Cock Eyed Jack's today (Camino) where the Raid of 1852 started.

Valley Miwok, who had experience with riding horses and herding cattle, were encouraged to make a big raid in the summer (Kaukati) of 1850.

The level open country around the towns of Diamond Springs and El Dorado (formally Mud Springs) was ideal for the Indian Warriors mounted on horseback to make a successful raid and escape in any direction necessary.

Many accounts said this raid was made by Maidu warriors but this seems to be in error. The main problem with this identification is that none of the raiders were ever captured or killed to be identified. The second reason this identity is in question, is because the local Maidu themselves said they were not responsible and gave several convincing facts to prove their innocence.

The raid started with a group of horse mounted warriors attacking Cockeye Jack Johnson's little settlement, present day Camino. Twenty years before it had been a Maidu settlement called Sa-Ski-An. The raiders took primarily live stock and were armed with guns and only a few bows. After hitting Cockeye Jack's they went around Pleasant Valley and hit Spring Valley then Mill valley. They attacked Hank's Exchange taking only loose cattle, however they did not shoot or go into the Miwok Rancheria at Hanks Exchange. In point of fact had the raiders been "Maidu" they would have shot up the "Miwok" Rancheria.

They shot at a miner in his cabin on a gulch near Martinez Creek, and then swept down into Ringgold, present day Big Cut Rd South of Weber Creek, shooting at cabins and anybody they saw.

They then hit the town of Diamond Springs (Banak'am Mo-lok Epakan) then Mud Springs (Present Day El Dorado) On-Cho-Ma.

Then the stories become confused; One account has the raiders turn their stolen stock 180 degrees around at today's Avansino Corner, then returned through many of the same areas they had shot up. They then crossed New Town Road to the forks of Webber Creek crossing and then North to the South Fork of the American River near the Old Brockless Bridge, just below today's Riverton on Highway 50. All this totally unobserved by anybody. Then this account had them driving these cattle and horses up Peavine Ridge toward Union Valley and "North or South" on Silver Creek.

My father Bill driving his Model T Ford

The other account (and the one supported by the local Maidu) was that the raiders went Southwest (basically along present day highway 49) and took the stolen stock down to dealers near Rancho Mureitta.

My Grandfather Bill and his Sawmill at Spanish Flat California

The local Maidu who lived in and around Chicken Flat in the 1930's often hung around my Grandfather's Sawmill in Spanish Flat. My Grandparent's home (where I now live) is located between Spanish and Chicken Flats (Hekeke-Toma). These Maidu were my grandparents neighbors. By the 1930's the Maidu's discussions about this "old history" were frank and all the details were pretty well known.

They made the case that the Indian Raiders of 1850 were not Maidu by several lines of reasoning. First; the raiders knew how to ride horses and were rather good at herding livestock. In 1850 almost none of the Maidu had any livestock or even knew how to ride a horse. They went on to point out that the raiders obviously knew where a horse-mounted party would be vulnerable because of where they did and did not attack. Camino could be easily hit from any direction and nothing would confine their escape. The fact they did not attack Pleasant Valley showed their experience with horses as there was no way to get out of Pleasant Valley that wasn't limited to a constricted pass with a steep timbered ridge on one side and a rocky cliff on the other. At certain places they would have been constricted to a pass only

Pleasant Valley is hemmed in with narrow passes that would restrict the horseback mounted raiders by steep timbered hillsides and rocky cliffs.

about one hundred yards wide, such as at the present-day Pleasant Valley Grange. At that and other places, a single American armed even with a shotgun or revolver, let alone a rifle, could have inflicted severe casualties on the raiders. The towns of Diamond Springs and El Dorado (Mud Springs) were located on open rolling land that would enable the raiders to maneuver and escape in any direction.

Second; They pointed out that the raiders did not attack the Indian Rancheria run by Julian Hanks (for whom Hanks Exchange is named). Julian Hanks, an associate of Sutter had hired local Miwok to run his operation. If the warriors in the raiding party had been Maidu they would have taken some revenge on the Miwok living there, yet these raiders did not.

For a prime example go to the Pleasant Valley Grange and note just how restricted the movement of livestock would be at this point. The Indian Raiders of 1852 must have already done scouting in the area and so did not attack Pleasant Valley.

Third; If the Raiders had been Maidu and had crossed the American River to Peavine Ridge, they could only get out of the Crystal Basin with the stolen cattle by going to the meadows around Wentworth Springs. From there they either had to go through the Rubicon Trail into the Lake Tahoe Basin (where they would have been spotted) or go West over Heartless Pass then down into the Georgetown Divide, where they

would also have been spotted.

If they had gone South and up the Silver Fork of the American River, they would have been going far out of Maidu country. This doesn't make much sense, considering how much thought had obviously gone into planning this raid.

The very findings of the Placerville Militia confirm the Maidu's belief that

Even a single man armed with a shotgun or revolver let alone a rifle could seriously hamper the raiders in these areas.

they were not the raiders.

In response to the raid three companies of militia were organized under Sheriff William Rogers numbering about 200 men. The little army did not employ any Indian scouts but consisted of self-described miners, gamblers, farmers and cutthroats.

They immediately went to Cockeye Jack Johnson's but didn't pick up the trail of the stolen livestock.

Even without Indian guides and if the militia were completely inept they still should have been able to follow a trail left by the herd of stolen livestock.

If, as the Maidu in the 1930's believed, the report of the raiders crossing back up the mountain North of the American River was a "Red Herring". This was probably dropped by somebody who stood to profit by the raid, then it makes sense that the Placerville Militia didn't pick up the Raider's trail.

The Militia then headed South toward Iowaville and Dogtown (today's Snows Road), crossed Pleasant Valley and then crossed the North Fork of the Co-sumnes River. They went to Somerset, Wisconsin Bar (Mt. Aukum Road) and down to Baker's Ford (the swimming hole by the two bridges on E-16). From

The Grey Eagle oak tree located on the trail from the Washoe camp to the Maidu camp near Balderston.

94

there they went down to River Pines and out the Shenandoah Valley eventually getting to Fiddletown. This entire operation reported to have killed one Indian.

The destination of the (Plains) Miwok Raiders was probably the area in the distance where the Rancho Seco Towers are now located. Open country and downhill from Mud Springs all the way to willing buyers for any livestock and or slaves they had acquired.

There was a report of a skirmish in which the Indian losses were heavy but the militia scout Bob Carson, Kit Carson's brother, called the report " a dam lie".

I have another report for 1850 (the Second Indian War of El Dorado County) that has Colonel Rogers (but adds a Major Kinney) and does not state where the action occurred. This report stated that Colonel Rogers and Major Kinney, at the head of the company attacked an Indian village in 1850. Major Kinney was killed by an arrow but the company managed to kill three or four Indians in the battle. However, I was unable to find anything else to corroborate this account.

Finally "Peg leg" Smith, a black man who had been a fur trapper and was familiar with the Indian lan-

Placerville California Today.   The site near Cool where Pico and his Piutes killed Avery.

guages, was hired by the militia to contact the Indians and make peace. The old man easily found the local Maidu Indians, who where more-than-willing to have peace, especially considering they didn't have anything to do with this raid.

Maidu Chiefs with the peace commissioners in 1851.

It seems highly probable that the Placerville Militia, under Sheriff Rogers, didn't find the trail of stolen cattle East near Camino, because the Miwok Raiders were busy herding said livestock down toward Rancho Murietta.

Another possibility does exist; The Maidu speculated that if the report of the Raiders going East was true, then they could have been Northern Paiute.

This is also a possibility as I found several stories about a white man named Avery who, depending on the version of the story, was either plowing a field or hunting near Pilot Hill when he was killed by a party of Paiute. The local Maidu helped the sheriff, A.L. Parker, a former Texas Ranger, track down the Paiute raiding party near Cool and apprehend them.

These Paiute were brought to trial before Judge J.D. Galbraith. During the trial, the leader stated that he was Chief Pico of the Paiute Tribe. The local Maidu pointed out these Paiute were nearly 150 miles from the nearest boundary with their homeland and were obviously on a slave-raid. Convicted of the murder and for stealing horses, the judge condemned Chief Pico and four of the warriors to death, but spared the youngest, a 12 year old boy. Then there are two versions of the story. In one version the 12 year old boy was allowed to go back to the Paiute. In the other, he was offered an education or to go back home and he chose to go to school.

The fact is that a party of Northern Paiute were caught in El Dorado County on a raid, in either 1850 or 1851. This demonstrates that the Raid in 1850 on Camino through Diamond Springs, could have been a Paiute effort. The Raiders would have gone up the Silver Fork of the American River and then taken Iron Mountain (Mormon Emigrant Trail) East to Carson Pass and over to their country in the Carson Valley and beyond. This was prior to the discovery of silver in the Carson Valley so the Paiute could have easily escaped detection.

This is also probable, as we do have records of several big meetings at Sly park (called Chu Ni in Miwok and Tgo No in Maidu) where tribes from Nevada and all over California gathered to trade. One estimate of the largest of these gatherings put the number of Indians attending at nearly 4,000. The Paiute traveling to these meetings would have used Carson Pass and been able to size up the possibilities of a raid into Camino to Diamond Springs.

The aftermath of the Indian Wars of El Dorado County.

The aftermath of these wars affected the Miwok and Maidu of El Dorado County very differently.

The State of California passed Assembly Bill No. 65, Protection of Indians, on April 22, 1850.

In section 7 the words were "If any person shall forcibly compel (an Indian) him or her to work or perform service against his or her will except as provided for in this Act (he or they) shall upon conviction be fined a sum not less than one hundred dollars nor more than five hundred dollars." At least it made enslaving Indians a crime even if the fine was rather limited.

By the 1870's the Miwok were living in the Cosumnes River canyon above Nashville located along Hwy 49.

Despite this law many Miwok were now being taken as slaves themselves by Mexicans and Americans. They were sold to Chinese, Chilean, Bolivian and Hawaiian miners as well as to fellow Americans and Mexicans. They were fair game now as even their former allies took them for slaves.

The remnant Miwok bands began to concentrate up in the steep canyon just East of the Confluence of the North and Middle forks of the Cosumnes River (U-Se-Si-Te).

The location of Louisville (Greenwood) in particular Poor's Store (foundation to the right of the stop sign.)

Men, John Steel, went down to Sacramento to get vaccinated. He returned and went to Chief Juan at Chicken Flats (Hekeke-Toma) and explained the benefits. He then used the quill of a hawks feather to vaccinate as many Maidu as he could, showing them how to vaccinate others. Many miners cons.

Chief Hunchup & Family
about 1906?
Sand Ridge   Cosumnes area

The Miwok were regarded as a nuisance and were allowed to live in the very steep canyon country where the forks of the Cosumnes River came together.

Many Miwok bands and the remnants of Charles Webbers Valley Miwok as well survivors from other areas came to the area located above present day Nashville located on highway 49 just South of El Dorado and North of the Amador County line.

The pictures on this page and over on the next page are of their largest round house in their community there above Nashville on Sand Ridge. At the turn of the century the primary Chief of the Miwok in this area was Hunchup who did his best. Shortly after the turn of the century there were several legal maneuvers intended to consolidate the Miwok or liquidate their lands. Chief Hunchup made the best decisions he could but he did not have the best legal minds or a cadre of mixed blood Cherokee to help him like the Maidu did.

Steel went to Sacramento and got vaccinated. He came up to Chicken Flat and showed them how to vaccinate themselves. The local Maidu took John Steel's advice and suffered only a few deaths from the epidemic. Jonathan Steele was later given a bow and a black fur quiver with arrows as a gift from Captain Juan.

Many Maidu integrated into American society; for example, John Henry Dodd married a Maidu girl in Chicken Flats (named Susan Lahie) where they planted an orchard and raised a large family. Jonathan Lauman, a 21 year old man originally from Norway, was living in Louisville (the intersection of Highway 193 and Spanish Flat Road) and married one of the Maidu girls from Chicken Flats (Hekeke-Toma). They settled where my place now sits and grew vegetables, fruit and also raised a large family. Some of their children talked to my Grandparents at the Sawmill.

Sometime in 1852 or 1853, depending on the version of the story, there was a "peace conference" called. Chief Juan and Coppa Hembo invited Jonathan Steel to come, apparently eight villages sent representatives from both the Maidu and Miwok peoples. The "Peace Conference" was held at a village two miles North West of "Moon Flat" (Columbia Flat). The village was surrounded by eight foot high poles, interwoven with brush, about one hundred yards in diameter. The ends of the stockade overlapped so that the entrances were not visi-

The site of the Village where the Maidu and Miwok worked out a peace between their tribes in 1852. Mr Steel was invited by the Maidu Chiefs to attend this conference and reported nearly 800 warriors were in attendance.

This Village hosted the eight day conference were the tribes settled their differences and worked on common problems facing their peoples. Coppa Hembo and Captain Juan were the primary Maidu leaders.

ble until one got very close.

The conference lasted eight or more days, during this time there was no consumption of alcohol. The Miwok made peace with the Maidu, they agreed that the situation had changed and they needed to bury the hatchet. They worked on several other issues including restricting alcohol consumption and legal issues. Jonathan Steele was asked questions about American laws and used as a reference by the tribal elders in making their decisions.

Jeff Barnhart beside the oak tree where he found the Republic of Bolivia Coin while raking leaves.

While the meetings went on many young men were playing a game similar to volley ball outside the wall of the village.

Some villages were abandoned in the next several years while new ones were built at the Fox, Davey and Wakefield Ranches in Garden Valley. These ranchers let the Maidu live on their land, often for nothing in return. The Maidu often worked on their farms and in the local mines and sawmills, as well as mining for themselves.

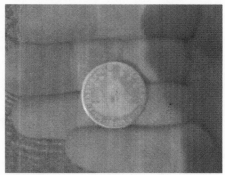

It should be noted that there were many ethnic groups in this area. We tend to think in terms of whites and Indians, but in fact the entire world had descended on California. Within the area of Garden Valley there were towns of French, German, Italian, Peruvian,

The Republic of Bolivia coin found by Jeff Barnhart.

Chelano, Columbian, Mexican, Bolivian, Chinese, and Hawaiian immigrants. All these ethnic groups came with their own contributions and problems.

For example; There was a small Chinatown located to the North side of Spanish Flat and Chicken Flat that had it's own opium den and Tong Gang members. To the North of Spanish Flat was Frenchman's Flat. The French Miners managed to get the Americans and Bolivians living around Spanish Flat so angry that a gun battle erupted with the French waving their tricolor flag in their camp and shooting until they were cut down.

Chief Hunchu's Band Ridge near 1904 Cosumnes area

For the Maidu the story was rather different. The luck of the draw put a large number of people of mixed Indian blood in their area who were more sympathetic to them.

The first gold rush in America was to the Old Cherokee Nation and those very people were removed in 1843 to the Indian Territory. To many Cherokee and mixed blood Indians this gold rush to California seemed the opportunity of their generation. The Cherokee had attained an eighty percent literacy rate before their removal and even if it was only in Cherokee they had several advantages over the other miners and soon owned the mines, stores and even the steam boats that worked the Sacramento and San Joaquin Rivers. One Cherokee names John Ridge (Yellow Bird) became the editor and writer for the Sacramento Bee and San Jose Herald. As such they helped the Maidu to integrate into American Society. An example of this was when a small pox epidemic broke out in 1852. One of Greenwood's men named John Steel was asked by Coppa Hembo to show them how to vaccinate themselves. Richard Steel showed them the technique at Hekeketoma (Chicken Flats) and from there a vaccination program was set up by Coppa Hembo that reached not only the Nisenan but Washoe as well.

The Bolivian town was located on what is now the Barnhart place; of interest, Jeff Barnhart was raking leaves a few years ago and found a Republic of Bolivia coin dated 1830 under his oak tree.

The Peruvians had a town called Peru up on what is now the Hakemoller Ranch.

The Hawaiians had come with John Sutter from Hawaii (then Called the Sandwich Islands) in 1839, they helped build John Sutters fort and run his operations. The Hawaiians had married local Miwok and Maidu women and had at least two settlements called Kanaka Towns. One was located at the end of Garden Park and the other off the North-West end of Deer Valley Road.

The site of the Kanaka Town off Garden Park Road today.

There were a number of free black people working mining claims and in mines around Kelsey, the Maidu called them "Charred People".

During the American Civil War a problem erupted at the one-room Kelsey schoolhouse, still located on the West end of Columbia Flat, the very site of the former head village of Po-No-Chitta–Toma. The children from Spanish Flat were pro-Confederacy, while the children from Kelsey were pro-Union and fights

The other town off Green Valley Rd.

were breaking out in class between these two factions. The Maidu children from Chicken Flats (Hekeke-Toma) were now grouped in the middle of the School room to keep the Kelsey kids separated from the Spanish Flat kids.

By this time the Maidu in Chicken Flats (Hekeke-Toma) had accepted many of the American holidays and combined them with their own. Most notably the Yakai winter festival was joined with Christmas and celebrated as a combined holiday.

Frank Lawyer with his meat cart in Chicken Flat about 1900 with the Maidu Widow Peggy who was paid a fine peace of meat to pose for this picture.

In this environment around 1860 (the stories vary) Coppa Hembo became the Chief of the Maidu living in Garden Valley and Mosquito.

Coppa Hembo and his wife Lucy lived in Chicken Flat (Hekeke-Toma) and had a home near the site of the village where the peace conference was held, now called Coppa Hembo Lane. One of Coppa Hembo's daughters married a well to do white man and had large family whose children integrated into society right away. Many local families are now descendants of Coppa Hembo.

One of the more colorful Maidu at Chicken Flat (Hekeke-toma) was Sam Pete. He was a good miner and was rather lucky at cards, but

My Grandfather Bill Nixon and Grandmother Lois Phillips Nixon

when asked how the game had been he would always say "Sam Beat". This was eventually turned into Sam Pete.

One local Maidu named Ed Drone worked for Old Man Poore who owned Poore's Store. The store was located at the intersection of Highway 193 and Spanish Flat Road, also known as Louisville.

Frank Lawyers home at Chicken Flat in 1905

Ed had a home next to Poore's house and worked for Poore at the store and across the street at the stables. One day a man who spoke Spanish (he could have been Mexican, Peruvian, Bolivian Ed didn't know) came riding down Spanish Flat road and went in to the store. Old Man Poore could speak some Spanish and the man asked for chewing tobacco, when Old man Poore turned his back to get the merchandise down from a shelf the man took a knife and opened up Old Man Poore's stomach so that his intestines fell out. The man then took the money from the cash register and ran out of the store, jumping on his horse, and

My Grandparents home in Spanish Flat During a community Hoedown, where all the neighbors came over with their fiddles and guitars, oboes and flutes with my Grandmother at the piano to have a good time.

Pictured above is my father's class picture of 1938 in front of the Kelsey School House. My father seated front right, had class mates of many ethnicity's. His classmates included Chilean, Metis, Maidu, Hawaiian, Black and Caucasian. My oldest son Bryan attended this same school-house for his Pre-school.

Pictured below is Margaret Kelly with her first class in 1886 she would retire from teaching at the Kelsey School when my father entered the second grade there. Chief Coppa Hembo often came to her classes both at the Greenwood school and the Kelsey school to speak. You can see from the picture below that the Greenwood school also had many Maidu children attending.

Margaret Kelly with the First Class at Greenwood School 1886

rode South toward Kelsey. Ed Drone and a
neighbor who had just rode up in his buckboard
went into the store and found Poore lying on the
floor, the neighbor ran out and took his buckboard
to get the doctor in Garden Valley. Ed put a clean
wet cloth over Poore's intestines to keep them
moist. The Doctor returned and with Ed's assistance put Poore's intestines back and stitched him
up.

My father as a school boy would go into Poore's
store on his way home from the Kelsey School
house and on several occasions saw Bill Poore
showing off the long scar and telling the story to
somebody.

Sam Pet at Chicken Flat

Coppa Hembo's widow Lucy moved from
Chicken Flats to Irish Creek at the old Burial Ground.
She died there in the winter (Ko-meni) of 1906. One
of the neighbors told Grandpa that the last "Cry" held at the old burial grounds
along Irish Creek was in 1905 and lasted three days.

He said an old Maidu named Ed Drone told him then, that would be the last
"Cry" because the "old Indians, all gone, young Indians ashamed, no cry".

As late as the 1930's when my Grandparents and dad lived out on the Old Ells
Place on Darling Ridge, there were still Maidu who would come to their house
then walk their trail toward castle Rock with the ashes of their dead.

The Maidu trusted my Grandfather, who was mostly Osage Indian and respected them. My grandmothers grandfather, Isaac Wheeler Phillips, had come
to California before the gold rush and married a woman from the Yana tribe. He
employed his wife's relatives and had many of them living on their farm. One
story in particular was that one day a group of Cheleno Cowboys came across
the river onto Issac's farm and shot his brother in law in the head.

Isaac had just purchased a new Winchester 1866 and he confronted the
Cheleno cowboys, who were used to single-shot muzzle-loading rifles. He told
them to get off his land and fired a warning shot, they figured he had just emp-
tied his gun, and came at him. Isaac then shot
their leader dead and fired another warning
shot. He got their attention, then told them that
if they ever crossed onto the Phillip ranch, hurt
or even annoyed any Yana, that he would per-
sonally hunt down and kill every damn one of
them. The Cheleno cowboys never did come
back.

The Nixon Trail (Maidu Trail)

Pictures of Isaac Wheelers Ranch and Saw Mill where my Grandmother grew up.

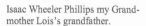

Isaac Wheeler Phillips my Grandmother Lois's grandfather.

He came to California before the Revolution and worked for John Sutter before the Gold Rush. He filed many mining claims but found that he could make more money hunting elk in the Sacramento Delta and selling the meat to the miners. He then bought a ranch in Lassen County and married a Yana Indian woman employing her family and friends on their ranch. He protected the Yana living on his ranch.

The Phillips Family Saw Mill on Bull Run today

Isaac then cut the bullet out of his brother in laws head and removed the broken piece of skull. He had seen a similar surgery where a bronze disk had been placed over the hole, but he only had a silver dollar. He had the silver dollar boiled clean and placed it over the hole in his brother–in-laws head before he sewed it up. The brother in law is pictured in the book "Men to Match My Mountains", by Irving Stone, pointing to the raised circle on his head, the photo was taken some ten years after the surgery.

My Grandmother had grown up on this family farm and sawmill near Oak Run East of Chico. When we go to Phillips Family reunions today it seems that nearly half the Yana people all use the last name of Phillips.

One day the US Forest Service came out and told Grandpa that they had named the trail going from his place to Castle Rock the "Nixon Trail, " and asked him to show them the trail so they could blaze it. Grandpa politely told them that it wasn't his trail and that it was not for use by white men. They didn't like his answer but they couldn't find the trail much past it's head. The old Forest Service maps show the Nixon trail but the line on the map was only their guess and it isn't very accurate.

My grandparents had pictures of some of the old Maidu in albums at the house. Durring World War II a Japanese Incendiary balloon landed in Kelsey Canyon and blew up. The resulting fire burned down Old Man Poor's Store, several other homes and our place.

My grandparents photos of these old people were lost but not their stories.

While the Maidu in Chicken Flat and Garden Valley integrated into American society it was much harder for the Miwok living South of Placerville.

From the beginning the Maidu and Washoe viewed the Americans as an asset while the Miwok viewed them as an enemy. After all the Americans had protected them from Miwok and Paiute slave raids.

This difference in attitude resulted in a very different experience for the Miwok versus the Maidu and Washoe.

Unlike the Maidu whose children were attending school by 1860, the Miwok in the South of El Dorado County were not allowed to go to public school until the 1880's.

While the Maidu and Washoe were productive members of the society, the majority of Miwok were either living on ranches like Hanks Exchange and Guttenburgers or on the two small rancherias, one on Snows Road and the other above Nashville. The reservation in Shingle Springs was too small to accommodate very many people, had no reliable source of water and was actually used by Kanaka (Hawaiian, Miwok and Maidu) descendents.

Putting Huuk (Chief) Coppa Hembo's achievement in perspective The Bald Hills War and the Maidu Trail of Tears

In order to understand just how much of achievement someone has made you need to see that in the context of what was happening around them. In the case of Chief Coppa Hembo and his people being able to attend school and integrate into society we should look at the conditions to both the North and South of his authority.

In 1858 California started what became known as the Bald Hills War. This War had two objectives, the first being to remove Native Tribes from the California Counties of Mendocino, Trinity, Humbolt, Klamath and Del Norte to make the land open for settlers. The second objective was to protect the Native peoples from contact with the settlers.

This war found the US Army, California Militia and California Volunteers fighting the Chilua, Lassik, Hupa, Mattole, Nongatl, Sinkyone, Tsnungwe, Wailaki, Whilkut and Wiyot peoples from 1858 until 1864. The Us Army found it extremely difficult to even find any Indians to fight in California's redwood rainforests and was soon reassigned to go back East to fight in the American Civil War but in fact they would see combat at the Battle of Apache Pass and be defeated by the forces of Cochise and Mangus Colorado. The California Militias could at lest find the native tribes to fight but being supported by their local counties lacked the resources and man power to comprehensively defeat the tribes. The majority of this conflict was handled by the California Volunteers who were supported by the State of California and could prosecute the war to the end of hostilities.

In point of fact some of these tribes did put up considerable resistance with the most noted of them being the Wailaki leader Lassic who was able to drive the settlers out of the Wailaki Homeland and defeat the forces sent against him. He would not surrender until July 31st 1862 in Humbolt County. Lassic would die later in January of 1863 at the hands of his captors.

All of these tribes were taken to the Nome Lackee Indian Reservation also known as the Round Valley Indian Reservation. This 36 square mile reservation was initially set up in a portion of the Yuki Tribes homeland but now had people from all these other tribes being forced to live with them even though several of these tribes were mortal enemies of the Yuki.

Add to this the Mill Creek Indians (part of the Yana tribe) as well as Concow, Little Lake, Nomelaki, Pomo, Cahto, Wailaki and Pit River peoples were also sent to the Round Valley Reservation.

Durring this conflict it was not uncommon for members of the Militia and Volunteers (a nominally Pro-Union State) to sell Indian women and children as slaves to make additional income.

Now due to the extremely rugged landscape cut by extremely deep river canyons that made up the Maidu homeland the Maidu were segregated into distinct bands rather than a single cohesive Tribe.

The Concow (Koncow) Maidu living in the vicinity of Chico were rounded up and then escorted by the US Calvary to the Rund Valley Reservation. The round up managed to get 461 Indians and started them on the Nome Cult Trail across the Sacramento Valley on August 28th 1863. Due to the extreme heat two of the 23 US Cavalrymen died from heat exhaustion while the poorly provisioned Indians died en-mass. Of the 461 who started what became known as the Maidu Trail of Tears only 277 would ever make it alive to the Round Valley Reservation.

Superintendent James Short was charged with helping get some 150 sick Indians who had been left beside the trail over a distance of fifty miles on to the reservation. In his report he was appalled to see that the feral hogs were eating the sick Indians beside the trail often before they had even died.

Once in the Round Valley Reservation the debate over whether it was the responsibility of the US Government or the State of California to provide the food for these people resulted in very few provisions arriving in an irregular schedule of questionable quality. As a result many of the 277 Concow Maidu who had made it to the Round Valley went back to their homes near Chico only to be rounded up and marched back to the Round Valley again.

This anti-Indian sentiment was still evident in 1929 when the local Baptist Preacher in Chico would not marry my Grandfather to my Grandmother because he would not marry an Indian to a white woman.

As another example Indians in the1930's could go in to see a movie in Auburn but had to sit in designated seats while South of the North Fork of the American River in Georgetown an Indian could go in to see a movie and sit where and with whom they wanted.

This difference was in part due to the fact that so many Cherokee came to the Georgetown and Placerville area during the Gold Rush. The other part of this was due to Chief Coppa Hembo's leadership and efforts. It was extremely lucky for the Hill Nissenan Maidu and Washoe living on the Georgetown Divide to have a leader who commanded authority whether speaking in English, Washoe, Nissenan or Spanish, had absolutely no fear but was not at all belligerent. In the opinion of many old timers, my Grandfather, father and I Coppa Hembo stands out as a great Native American Leader.

Indian Horse traders at Newtown   (E-Kele-Pa-Kan)

E-Kele-Pa-Kan (Newtown)

Pictured above and below are Shoshone often referred to in Newtown as Pinyon Indians.

    The Gold Rush also opened up business opportunities for Indians: for example the Shoshone Horse dealership located just East of Placerville at Newtown.   Sometime before 1872 the Italian community of Newtown (between Pleasant Valley and Placerville) was the location for Shoshone horse traders to do their business.

They were called Pinyon Indians and were under the leadership of Chief Hila; from their description and names they were Shoshone or possibly Bannock. In the summer they would bring wild horses from Nevada over Carson Pass down to Newtown. Here they built corrals and several cedar bark dwellings at a place called Grayston, located 100 yards up stream from the old Hesque barn called Rug Gulch. They would break the mustangs and sell them locally. They impressed the local families as they were tall athletic people who had incredible skill in horsemanship.

While they were in residence, Chief Hila's sister (known as Sarah) was well-known for her ability to help people with herbs and her bone setting skills. Many people from all over Pleasant Valley and the Newtown area sought her out.

The unofficial Justice of the Peace at Smith Flat, John Ringer, said of these Indians. "They paid their bills, asked no favors, spoke good English and were honest and law abiding". He wished the white men around there were half as honest and hard working.

In the Italian community there was one young man named Gigio who boasted that he had stolen money from his parents to come to America. In the opinion of the community he was rather worthless. Twice the community had raised enough money to send Gigio to San Francisco to get a job. Both times Gigio returned in a few weeks out of money and boasting of the good time he had enjoyed.

Most people in the Newtown area went to the Pinyons corrals on Sundays to watch the Indians work their horses. It was much like a rodeo and families came to watch the horsemanship.

One particularly hot September afternoon, Gigio showed up at the corrals playing with old man Simons revolver that he had pilfered from the mans cabin. One of the Pinyon girls was working a horse and, on all accounts, she was very attractive, Gigio hollered obscene things to her in Italian and what little English he knew but she ignored him. He then went over, grabbed the reins of her horse in one hand and her thigh with his other hand. She slapped him in the face with her riding quirt and just as quickly Gigio pulled out the revolver and shot her twice, killing the young woman. Gigio immediately began to ask the other men to get their guns and protect him, as the Indians would be sure to kill him. Instead several of the burly Italians knocked him down and kept him from getting away.

Within an hour or so, Chief Hila and eight of his sons came riding into Newtown, where Sheriff John Ringer was waiting to negotiate as best he could. Chief Hila's oldest son dismounted stiffly and walked up to John and they talked for nearly an hour as to what should be done. While they were talking, Gigio, who was on the ground crawled away. Old Man Simon watched Gigio crawl off then he went to the ravine where Gigio was hiding. Several other Italians saw this as well soon there was a rifle shot. The Italians came back out of the nearby ravine carrying the body of Gigio with a large hole in his head. They dropped the body unceremoniously on the dirt road and spit on the body before stepping back.

John Ringer and Hilia's son then solemnly shook hands. The Shoshone rode away toward Greystone in the moonlight. (Greystone was later called Creighton Valley (S16, T10N, R12E,) located on the North side of the South Fork of Weber Creek.) The Indians gathered up their goods and rode back to Nevada, never to return. All the old timers agreed that it was a great loss to Newtown and the Pleasant Valley area.

The Plains Miwok (those living in the Sacramento and San Joaquin Valleys) had been in John Sutter's way. Between 1839 and 1841 he played-off one group against another to gain control of the lower Sacramento Valley. Many had been enslaved and sent to Mission San Jose as well as the Mexican Ranchos and the Mercury Mines of New Idra and New Almaden; All this, as well as recurrent outbreaks of malaria starting in 1833 had decimated their numbers. From an estimated population of 17,000 in 1770 they had been reduced to 6000 by 1848 and only 100 by 1880. In one hundred and ten years they

Part of the route taken by the Plains Miwok Slave Raiders

went from 17,000 to 100 people!

Another unknown number of Plains Miwok survivors were those who had married Kanakas (John Sutter's Hawaiian's). This number is impossible to determine as Hill Miwok and some Maidu also married Kanakas.

The Coast Miwok had taken an even greater loss.

Coast Miwok had greeted Sir Francis Drake in 1579. In 1783 the Spanish began taking Coast Miwok for labor on the Mission San Francisco de Asis now known as Mission Dolores. By 1817, large numbers of Coast Miwok were also being taken by Mission San Jose. In 1834 the Franciscan missionaries were replaced as all the mission lands were ceded to Californios. The Miwok were then forced to live in servitude on the ranchos, with the population nearly all restrained in the tight confines of the ranchos, a small pox epidemic in 1837 decimated their numbers.

In 1843 California Governor Micheltorena granted two sq. leagues of land, known as Rancho Olompali for the remaining free Coast Miwok under their leader Camilo Ynitia. However, in 1852 most of the land was acquired by James Black, of Marin. With only 1,480 acres left, called "Apalacocha" operated by Camilo's daughter who eventually lost this as well, leaving this group of Miwok with nothing.

Another group of Coast Miwok (Mission Indians) who were able to get some land in the California takeover of church properties. In 1835 they got 20 leagues (80,000 acres) located from Nicasio to Tomales Bay. By 1850, they had only one league of this land left. This was done by Californios and Mexicans simply confiscating their land. By 1880 after many had been taken for slaves, there were only 36 Coast Miwoks left. They were forced to leave, as Marin County curtailed funds to Indians not living at the Poor Farm for "Indigent" peoples.

By 1880 there were only 60 Coast Miwok people left of both the free and mission Indians. This doesn't count those who were enslaved on ranchos or the offspring of intermarriages who were no longer identified as tribal peoples. Several of these Coast Miwok families made a living by commercial fishing until 1972, when it became no longer profitable and they had to leave.

In the end they were left with nothing, no reservation, no casino, no land, nothing!

The Southern Sierra Miwok (who lived along the Merced and Chowchilla Rivers and Mariposa Creek) and the Central Sierra Miwok (who lived along the Stanislaus and Tuolumne Rivers) fared the best of all the Miwok populations. They lived at elevations above the Malaria carrying mosquitoes and had not been living in the heart of the Gold Rush area. They had been too remote for the Missions to get very many of them and difficult for Mexicans to catch and enslave for their Ranchos.

A large number of Miwok managed to live in the area from Sheep Ranch to Murphys in several Rancherias, and private farms.

A large Miwok Rancheria located next to Murphys California was brought to the point of conflict. Miners from Murphys were going out to the Miwok Rancheria at night to rape and molest Miwok women and girls. The Miwok were frustrated with the lack of response from the sheriff and were ready to take matters into their own hands when a force of residents from Murphys confronted them. Only the actions of the Miwok Chief defused the situation. Some years later three school boys stoned a crippled Miwok girl to death beside the road near Murphys and were never even arrested for it. This example shows the general attitude that was in place well up into the 1930's.

Those Miwok living in the Yosemite Valley continued to live in a quasi free state longer than any other group. The free-range livestock, and their herders caused the biggest reduction of their numbers. Many were caught and sold as slaves or concubines, while others intermarried with the stockmen, generating a population of mixed bloods who assimilated fairly easily and greatly assisted their full blood relatives.

The Maidu to the North.

The Maidu to the North of the Georgetown Divide had a different experience. While in Placerville and Georgetown they were treated the same as whites, in Auburn they were required to sit in certain areas for example, up until the 1930's they were required to sit in a specific balcony in the back of the movie theater. The California Indians finally did get US citizenship in 1924 and with it the right to vote.

The Maidu had always lived in Plumas County particularly the Hum Bug Valley (Tos-Ma). They felt it was blessed because there were no rattlesnakes in the valley. There still aren't rattlesnakes in this valley. The wasn't any gold but the land was good for ranching and had timber, so fewer white settlers came in at a slower rate.

These Maidu would work on the local ranches as field hands and on farms. Some specialized in making tool handles and baskets or rendering bear grease for cooking lard and lubricating grease.

The Maidu and Pit River tribes never went to war against the invaders, but were still seen as subhuman. One woman (Mary) remembered that as a little girl a group of cowboys rode into the Indian villages along Hat Creek in the Dixie Valley. The cowboys shot some people, burned the homes and kidnapped the women and children. This woman was only about eight years old when the cowboys roped her and others. They were taken to Big Meadows (present day Chester California) where they were auctioned off. She remembered that the cowboys got a good horse and some gold for her and she was bought by Fred Thomas. The man had a wife and several children, some of whom were just as old as she was. She was a slave and worked for them, then one day after she reached puberty he began raping her. She was called his second wife and had children by him. She thought of running away but didn't know if there was anything left to go back to. She would not be able to return to Hat Creek until she was a middle aged woman with many children by Fred Thomas. This was a common way for cowboys to make some extra money when the cattle didn't need working and there was nothing else better to do. Many young women were sold like this while the older boys or submissive men were sold to work in mines or ranches.

One Maidu fellow named Bert Thomas was so irritated by the actions of the local cowboys with his girl cousins that he dressed like a girl and when a local cowboy grabbed him he decked the pervert and knocked him out. The cowboy could not let it be known that a "Little Indian Girl" had clobbered him but it made him quit grabbing the little girls.

Beverly Ogle's family story correlates with many of the experiences my family above Chico had for the same time period. Many of the cowboys were men who had come to California from Mexico and South America to "go get rich quick" in the gold fields but later turned to ranch labor to make a living. They operated just as they had in their native countries and took it for granted that the local Indians were available to be taken as slaves or shot up for entertainment. This wasn't an "Indian War" per se as it had nothing to do with the local government let alone the US Government. If the Indians resisted or struck back it was then declared a "war" and the government would organize an army to defeat them.

Those who were rounded up by a government army were herded off to the Round Valley Indian Reservation located in the Coast Range Mountains, far from their home lands and everything they knew.

Many tolerated the violence and tried their best to make a living with the White settlers. Some of them let the Indians live at best as communities on their land, or at worst, as second wives or slaves.

A Yosemite Miwok woman and her baby from an old Post Card 1900

Yosemite National Park

Because they did not go to "War" many of these people's descendants are not recognized as Indians by the U.S. government, as such, they have no status or reservations. They often take it as a bit insulting when it is assumed today that Indians get free money and have their own casino's which isn't really the case.

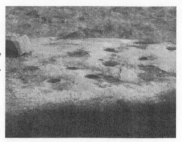

As an example of the "other way" let me use the Paiute of Pyramid Lake Nevada. The Paiute were living along the Truckee River below present-day Reno, Nevada, to Pyramid Lake.

In May 1860 a group of miners ran-down five Paiute girls and took them to Williams Station just North of Virginia City, where the girls were raped repeatedly. The angry fathers came to Williams Station and killed the rapists and burned the place to the ground.

In response, the miners organized a force of 105 men, including the now famous Show Shoe Thompson, and led by a Major Ormsby. When the troops approached the Indians the Paiute came out to talk with white flags clearly visible. SnowShoe Thompson as well as others, verified that it was the troopers who fired on the Indians carrying the white flags who started the battle. Major Ormsby lead a charge and was killed along with 75 of the troops. SnowShoe Thompson was among those who were able to make it away from the battle alive.

This defeat caused the miners of Virginia City, Nevada to form an enormous force of troops and militia raised from as far away as Sacramento. This new army closed in on the Paiute, and on June 2, 1860 they defeated the Paiute in the second battle. The Paiute fought long enough for the women and children to pull together and escape. The Paiute split up into different groups and fled leaving the "White Army" with the battlefield.

Even this "Victory" had inflicted far more casualties to the whites than the Paiute, so both sides considered it a "victory". After this, and many other battles, the Paiute were finally federally recognized and now have the Pyramid Lake Reservation.

The Modoc

The Modoc Tribe of Northern California and Southern Oregon were ethnically and linguistically the same as the
Klamath Tribe. The Klamath tribe was
primarily a fishing based culture with
extensive fishing wheels, screens and
nets deployed to make full use of the

Captain Jack Modoc Leader (Keintposes)

resources available to them. Even before the coming of the Europeans the
demand for smoked fish and other products had made the tribe wealthy and
powerful.

To increase production the Klamath began to have slaves. As the wealth
and standard of living, increased the tribe desired more slaves. For those
Klamath living in the upper reaches of the river systems a great deal of
goods and wealth could be had by supplying slaves to those parts of the
tribe closer to the coast. The desire to get slaves took these Klamath further into the interior and eventually to the area where they were living when
John Fremont explored the area in 1843.

During this time they made their living in an area with few resources but
otherwise was productive in the transport of slaves taken from tribes further
East. The Modoc could go out and capture slaves from
the Paiute and Shoshone, then upon delivery to the
Lower Klamath Tribe would have a big party with supplies enough to carry them through the next year with
ease.

Klamath people

The arrival of the horse to the Paiute changed them from
prey to predator; as now they were looking for slaves to
sell to the New Mex cans and Mexicans to exchange for

more horses.

This changed the dynamic and soon the Modoc were mounted as well and locked in a bitter turf war with the Paiute. By the mid 1840's this was an all out conflict with the Paiute winning many of the major fights but the Modoc still managing to kidnap a number of Paiute women and children for slaves.

The coming of the Americans was seen as an invasion by the Modoc but also a source of horses which could even the odds against the Paiute.

Winema (Toby Riddle) standing between an Indian agent and her husband Frank (on her left) with other Modoc women in 1873

In the Fall of 1852 Captain Jack's Father led an attack on a wagon train of settlers at a place later called "Bloody Point" along the shore of Tule Lake.

Of the 65 people in the wagon train, all but three were killed. One man escaped by hiding in the thick tules and later reported the attack. The other two survivors were two little girls, one with blond hair the other with red hair.

These two girls were soon bought and sold by many Modoc to be used as prostitutes. The girls brought so much money and were in such demand, that several years later a Modoc woman (who was mad that her husband had spent so much for them) pushed one over a cliff and then killed the other girl with an axe. During the period from 1845 to 1872 some 300 white men women and children were killed by the Modoc.

An example of a Fishing Wheel

Warm Springs Indian Scouts who were invaluable in tracking and fighting the Modoc.

Modoc War

In 1854 the warfare was so intense that freighters refused to ship goods through the region to supply Jacksonville, Oregon, and Yreka, California.

In 1864 a meeting with the tribes was negotiated to establish a peace treaty. Some 710 Klamath tribesmen, as well as

Soldiers Recovering the Bodies of the Slain May 3, 1873

339 Modoc, and 22 Snake River Indians attended. The group finally agreed that if the government set up a reservation on the Klamath River

the tribes would stop fighting.

The plan was good at the time of the negotiation but an external factor would soon render the reservation plan impossible.

With the Union victorious in the American Civil War, the Emancipation Proclamation was extended to include those slaves living in Union occupied areas. This set free those slaves living in Washington DC and by logical extrapolation, those living on the Klamath reservation.

The ratio of slaves to former masters was 7 to 3 (70% had been slaves). With their freedom the former slaves began to murder their former masters and take control. When the Modoc came in for their free food and supplies they were not greeted by a welcome party, but instead met by a group of people who intensely hated them. The Modoc quickly found that they could not expect to survive let alone get any free food or supplies from the Klamath Reservation.

The Modoc returned to their own territory along the Lost River where they demanded the settlers pay them rent for living on their land. The settlers complained, but most paid "Rent" to the Modoc. The Government tried to persuade the Modoc to return to the reservation; with efforts in 1865 through 1867 that all failed.

The Modoc had also found a new source of revenue. They would capture the girls and women of other tribes and use them as prostitutes in the mining camps. Some Modoc women seeing, just how much money could be made became prostitutes themselves. Some Modoc Women had married white men, but this was soon rejected, as the tribe would lose its women and future sources of such revenue.

Captain Jack (Keintposes) was convinced to return to the Klamath reservation in 1868, with the government promise that former slaves wouldn't even ridicule him. He left after only three months.

Captain Jack did promise to stop having his people collecting "Rent" from the settlers and cease prostitution in the mining camps, if the Government would build them a Reservation on Lost River. This was considered but the lava fields surrounding the area meant significant time and expense as well as the estimated loss of a considerable number of wagons to maintain this reservation, with a limited budget the Government decided it was just too expensive.

The Indian Affairs Superintendent T.B. Odeneal decided the Modoc had done enough and ordered Captain James Jackson with 40 troopers of the 1st cavalry, to remove the Modoc to the Klamath Reservation (by force if necessary)!

The Army caught the Modoc camp by surprise and began to disarm the Modoc. Scarface Charley and Lieutenant Boutelle drew on each other and fired their guns, both missing. The fight was on. The Modoc shot eight troopers, while the troopers shot one Modoc. The troopers didn't try to pursue and the Battle of Lost River ended.

The Modocs in Their Stronghold, an 1873 wood engraving

The Modoc had announced to the settlers that if the Army tried to put them on the Klamath Reservation or if the settlers refused to pay their "Rent" they (the Modoc) would kill every settler in the basin. Hooker Jim and his group then did just that and killed 17 settlers in the area, taking their supplies and horses.

"Medicine Rock" On this formation the Modoc placed their medicine flag made of a Mink skin and hawk feathers, it also anchored the Red Rope.

The army spent more than a month and a half getting forces organized; meanwhile the Modoc, who believed they could not be beaten in the Lava country, prepared for war.

The War in the Lava beds made for innovation , a mule-back litter.

The Modoc attacked the Army ammunition wagon train on December 21, 1872, killing two and wounding five more troopers.

The Modoc let the US Army know they were on the shore of Tule Lake and waited for them to attack. When the Army finally arrived they were confident they could sweep the Modoc. With 225 regular troops and 104 volunteers plus two howitzers. They moved on the Modoc on January 16, 1873. The US Army attacked the forty or less Modoc Warriors, who were nearly impossible to see because a low fog was in the area, and the advancing US Troops were decimated. The ground that had appeared level was full of hollows and sharp lava rocks where the Modoc could hide. The attack was beaten off. Even before Colonel Wheaton ordered retreat most of the surviving troopers were headed back.

The Army had lost 37 men, while not a single Modoc had been touched. Captain Bernard said his men would rather get twenty years in Leavenworth, Kansas than attack that mess again.

The US Army went to the neighboring Indian Reservations and asked for volunteers to track and fight the Modoc; to their surprise, they were almost overwhelmed by the number of volunteers, especially from the Paiute on the Warm Springs Reservation. Little did they realize that most of these men hated the Modoc with a vengeance and would be hard to reign back.

Meanwhile the Modoc celebrated and were confirmed in their belief that the White Man could not beat them in their country. They had cattle herds in basins surrounded by lava and a cavern with ice where they could keep meat frozen indefinably.

The Army regrouped and sent for General Canby commander of the Department of the Columbia. Once General Canby arrived he tried to negotiate with Captain Jack but the idea of a reservation on Lost River was still the Modoc demand. Although Captain Jack was in favor of peace the other chiefs felt that it was just a plan to get them out of their stronghold where they would be hung. They convinced Captain Jack on a plan to murder the peace commission.

The US Army learned to fight using fortifications made of lava rocks and to slowly take ground in a form of trench warfare.

The Morning of April 11,1873 the Peace Commission met in a tent. Boston Charley and Bogus Charley walked the interpreters Frank and Toby Riddle to the site where Captain Jack , Schonchin John, Hooker Jim, Ellen's Man George, Shacknasty Jim and Black Jim were waiting. Just a little after noon Captain Jack jumped up yelling "At-we!" which was the signal for Barncho and Slolux, who had been hiding in the brush, to come running to him with armloads of rifles.

General Canby asked what was the meaning of this as Captain Jack turned a revolver on him and pulled the trigger. The revolver misfired but Jack thumbed the hammer back again and shot the general in the left eye. The attack killed General Canby and Mr. Thomas. The Indian Agent Meacham had been shot three times and scalped but would later recover.

Dyar and Riddle escaped while Toby Riddle stayed and helped to save Meacham by shouting " the Soldiers are coming!" The dead and wounded white men were stripped of their clothes and left for dead.

Another group of Modoc came out of their stronghold under a white flag of truce and met Lt. W.L. Sherwood and killed him.

It had been the Modoc plan to kill all of the Army leadership but several escaped. The effort managed to alienate the Eastern Church Groups who had been supporting the Modoc on religious grounds.

The Second Battle for the Stronghold

After the soldiers saw the mutilated bodies of the General and the others some were ready to attack immediately but Colonel Gillem held them back. Colonel Gillem was waiting for the Warm Springs Indian Scouts under Donald McKay to arrive. He reasoned that these men could make the difference in a battle like this.

Many people have wondered why the Indian Scouts were so eager to fight the Modoc. A single story about one of these Warm Springs Paiute Scouts is very revealing.

124

The story was that this Indian was one of the Scouts who was photographed and possibly Loa-kum-ar-nuk, but that can not be determined. As they story goes the scouts were camped one evening when an officer, with several soldiers, asked them why they fought for the white men against the Modoc? This man revealed that he was captured as a young boy with his mother, grandmother, and older sister by the Modoc. They were marched hard and his grandmother fell breaking her leg so she was left to die. When they arrived at the Klamath village, the Modoc sold him and his mother, sister and several other Paiute as slaves. There was a big party and the new owner, to show his wealth, allowed his guests to rape this man's older sister. He believed that she had not reached puberty yet and after several men her uterus prolapsed. She died slowly, over a period of days, with her uterus hanging out of her body. Several years later the man's mother was killed during another party. The American Civil War and Abraham Lincoln's Emancipation Proclamation set him free so he left the Klamath Reservation to be with his own people on the Warm Springs Reservation. Then Loa-kum-ar-nuk asked the officer why he had only been issued five rounds of ammunition? The officer told him the government didn't want them to kill all the Modoc. His story was not unique and all of the Scouts were more-than-eager to get even with the Modoc.

Genereal Canby

The peace Commision Tent were the murders took place.

With the arrival of the Warm Springs Indian Scouts, the attack was planned for April the 12th. With 675 troops and Indian allies the force was set to attack on two fronts. The experienced troops advanced and built stone fortifications as they slowly inched forward. It was a World War I-style trench system such as some had experienced in the Battle for Vicksburg a few years earlier.

Loa-kum-ar-nuk, a Paiute from the Warm Springs Indian Reservation who volunteered to help the US Army find and fight the Modoc. Like many of his companions he had deeply personnel reasons for wanting to fight the Modoc. As a result the Indian Scouts were limited to five rounds each.

This tactic surprised Captain Jack and the other Modoc, who were only able to kill three soldiers and wound another six. On the 16th of April the commands of Mason and Green joined forces in the South and built stone fortifications from which they beat back several Modoc attacks without losing a single man. The artillery was trying to break the Modoc but in reality was only supplying the Modoc with more powder and lead from the recovery of the unexploded shells.

Finally, with the aide of the Warm Springs Scouts, the Army was able to cut the Modoc off from the lake and its water. Little did the Army know that the Modoc had water and ice, in several caverns inside their stronghold, so this achievement was not a great loss to the Modoc; however the Army had crossed the Red Tule Rope that the Modoc Medicine Man (Curley Headed Doctor) had placed around the stronghold and had said the Army would not be able to cross. The Warm Springs Piute began heckling the Modoc that they were using the Red Tule Rope for firewood and that the Modoc Medicine was broken. That day the first Modoc was killed while trying to open an artillery shell. Prior to that the unexploded shells had been used by the Modoc for powder and the casings melted down for bullets.

That evening with the Army slowly closing in and their Medicine broken, the Modoc decided to escape to the South through a tunnel to the Schonchin Lava Flow.

The Modoc escaped completely without the Army realizing it until noon the following day. The Army quickly began building fortifications of their own to prevent the strongholds possible recapture by the Modoc, while the Scouts were deployed to find out where the Modoc went.

April the 17th had been a defeat for the Army as the Modoc had escaped with the Army taking eighty five casualties.

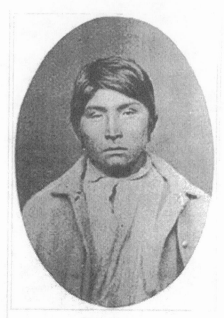

Boston Charley in 1873

After two days Colonel Gillem got word from Captain Perry, that the Modoc were still in the lava flows and the Warm Springs Scouts had located the Modoc in one of the larger flows. Colonel Gillem wanted a howitzer placed in a position where it could pound this new position. He dispatched 66 men under Captain Thomas on April 26, with twelve Warm Springs Scouts. However the scouts were delayed and did not accompany them.

The Modoc figured out what the unit was trying to do and dispatched about 12 warriors under Scarfaced Charley to ambush the 66 soldiers. When the soldiers stopped for lunch the Modoc attacked, nearly half the soldiers fled but the other half were hammered. The Modoc managed to kill all five officers and twenty soldiers, wounding another sixteen. There would have been more soldiers killed except for Scarfaced Charley's mercy. He hollered out to the troopers late in the afternoon "All you fellows that ain't dead yet had better go home. We don't want to kill you all in one

day." The Modoc had won another Battle called the "Thomas-Wright Massacre".

The Modoc moved South and went to Dry Lake, where they found the camp of Captain Hasbrouck. The Modoc crept in on the night of May 9th, to attack the camp in the morning of the 10th. The soldiers took heavy casualties before regrouping and actually attacking the Modoc positions. The Warm Springs Scouts, who were camped not far away, came up behind the Modoc and put them in a deadly crossfire. The Modoc lost their pack animals and were shattered but managed to make it to Big Sand Butte, three and a half miles away, to regroup.

The Army had five more killed and five more wounded, but the battle had shaken the Modoc, who now questioned Captain Jack's leadership. The group split into two factions. The splinter group headed for Sheep Mountain while Captain Jack and 33 warriors remained until May 16th before they also retreated.

Scarfaced Charley ,the Commanding officer of the Modoc Forces at the Thomas/Wright Battle.

The splinter group, led by Hooker Jim was finally tired out and surrendered on May 22nd at John Fairchild's Ranch. After their surrender, Hooker Jim, Bogus Charley, Shacknasty Jim, and Steamboat Frank volunteered to guide the Army to where the die hards were hiding out. With their directions, the Warm Springs Scouts were soon hounding the remaining Modoc. Captain Jack (Keintposes) finally gave up to Major Trimble on June 1, where he was reported to have said that his legs had given out. Curley Headed Jack had taken a revolver and shot himself in the head, rather than facing the possibility of being hung.

In the end, the war had cost the US Government far more than the requested reservation on Lost River.

General Davis started the immediate construction of gallows from which to hang the Modoc ring leaders when he received a stop order. President Grant declared that only those who had violated the flag of truce could be held responsible. The other leaders were instead prisoners of war.

Lela, daughter of Modoc Chief Yellowhammer pictured after the Modoc War.

Only Schonchin John, Boston Charley, Black Jim, Barncho, Captain Jack and Slolux were required to stand trial with all of them getting the sentence of death by hanging.

However, President Grant commuted the sentences for Barncho and Slolux.

Then on October 3, 1873 these leaders were hung with the whole Modoc Tribe watching. The whole tribe was then shipped off to the Quapaw Reservation in The Indian Territory (Oklahoma) .

Below a picture of the period showing the Modoc

Captain Jacks Family; Lizzie, young wife, Mary, his sister, Old wife and Daughter

This firing position was used by the troopers to fend off repeated Modoc attacks from the West but was exposed to fire from the Modoc Warriors positioned on the East side of Captain Thomas's command.

Pictured above is a facsimile of the Medicine Flag erected a short distance from where the original one stood during the battle.

The stronghold was only abandoned after the Paiute Warriors managed to take the Medicine Flag and burn the Red Tule Rope made by the Modoc Medicine Man (Curley Headed Doctor) . This was followed by a Modoc Warriors being killed as he opened up an unexploded artillery shell proving that the medicine had been broken.   The Modoc slipped out of the stronghold to the South completely unobserved. It would take the Army a full day and a half to determine that the Modoc had escaped.

The Warm Springs Paiute warriors were sent out to find the Modoc. They determined that the Modoc were still in the lava beds in the area later designated the Schonchin lava flow.

The Army began to probe the lava flow and were soon fighting the Modoc in the area of "Devils Homestead".   In an effort to bring their artillery into an effective position Colonel Gillem ordered Captain Thomas and 66 men with five officers to take the howitzer around to the South of the Modoc position.

The memorial to General Canby "Canby's Cross" located where he fell dead from Captain Jack.

My son Jacob stands at the site of Army Operations during the Modoc War known as Gillems Camp. Located to the West of the Modoc Fortress al-
long

Pictures below on the left is my son Jacob in a small cave located on the Southern defensive line where Modoc Warriors took shelter from falling artillery before jumping back out of the small cave and firing at the advancing federal troops. The Modoc fortress was compared to the defensive works at Vicksburg by Federal officers.

Pictured above are my three sons in the natural trench/ line of the eastern face of Captain Jacks Stronghold. The depth of these trenches enabled the Modoc to reload their muzzle loading guns in safety before climbing back to their firing positions. These trenches interlock and provided the Modoc Warriors the ability to move from one zone to another to concentrate their fire on new attacks with out being exposed.

The ground appears level from the outside and these trenches so enabled the warriors to move unseen that the Federal Officers and men estimated fall greater numbers of Modoc than there actually were.

Pictured to the left is the actual location of the Medicine Flag. My son Jacob stands on top of the rim of the line facing the cattle corrals where the Modoc kept cattle during the battle.

In point of fact on many occasions, the Modoc would bar-B-Q beef and let the smell waft over the Federal troops they had pinned down. The Modoc would comment on how delicious the beef was and ask how hungry and thirsty the soldiers were.

With cattle as well as other food supplies they had previously stored in the Stronghold the Modoc were more than prepared for a prolonged siege.

In point of fact the Modoc had used this fortification many times before against attacks from other Indian tribes forces. Against these forces the problem of keeping the attackers supplied had always resulted in them breaking off their sieges before the Modoc's supplies gave out. With this history the fortification was well supplied long before the war. The fortification was not only known to the Paiute who were being used by the Army as scouts but all of the US Army intelligence about this fortification had been provided by them as well.

Pictured above and to the left is a reenactor with an example of the army rifle used during the Modoc War. The Spencer Rifle was a repeating rifle with a seven round magazine located in the stock of the gun that was cycled by means of a lever as seen in the open position in these pictures. The cartridge used was the .56/50 Spencer. This round had enormous knockdown power and was effective out to around three hundred yards, although due to the sights and state of manufacture actually striking a man sized target consistently was limited to around one hundred yards.

Pictured here is the location of the Thomas/Wright Battlefield. The lava field provided excellent cover for the Modoc to ambush the Army Units and pin them down. My friend Brian Hindman in authentic uniform is shown in positions where the battle was fought.

Colonel Gillem ordered Captain Thomas not to leave with out a unit of 14 Warm Springs Paiute Scouts. These scouts had been on a mission to the East and did not meet up with Captain Thomas. He had left and was approaching the designated artillery position only to be ambushed by the Modoc.

 The Army force of 66 men and five officers was decimated with all five officers being killed, twenty of the enlisted men killed and the wounding another sixteen. While at the start of the battle some soldiers had escaped the rest were being slowly killed off and had no chance of escape.

Late in the day the leader of the Modoc Forces named Scarfaced Charley decided to have mercy on the soldiers, he hollered out to the remaining army men, "All you fellows that ain't dead yet had better go home. We don't want to kill all of you in one day". This gave the wounded and able bodied men the opportunity to retreat but they left their artillery and this retreat enabled the Modoc to gather up their Spencer rifles and a large supply of their ammunition as well as the ammunition for the artillery which the Modoc could convert for use in their own Muzzle loading rifles.

 The war would continue but every future army troop movement would be made with the Paiute Scouts to prevent disasters like this.

In the next battle it was the Paiute who saved the soldiers from another disaster by going around an attacking force of Modoc and destroying the Modoc's supply train of ammunition.

The Modoc started their ambush from this lava formation which had funneled Captain Thomas and his unit of sixty six men into a narrow flat space some twenty yards wide. The only cover inside this flat was provided by two juniper trees one of which is pictured below to the left.

The artillery had been hand drawn due to the rough terrain and was abandoned approximately five yards in front of this tree.

The troopers who held out had to get in close to the Modoc to get behind the lava boulders but were subject to cross fire from the Modoc moving into positions in the lava formation to the East of them. It was this combination that provided the Modoc with their last large victory in the Modoc War.

The American South West

The migrations of people into (and out of) the Southwestern portion of the United States are now fairly well known. The "Cliff Dwellers" or Anasazi were an agriculturally based people who were driven out of much of the area by prolonged droughts and the invasion of the "Navajo peoples". The remnant of the original peoples are represented by the Tohono O'dham, Pima, Papago, Hopi and Zuni. South in Mexico are the Seri, Tarahuamara, Mayo and Yaqui.

The Navajo population was slowly moving South into the American Southwest starting in about the twelfth century. The leading edge of this population that came into contact with the indigenous peoples was forced to either fight them or assimilate them. This edge began to be ethnically and culturally distinct from the main population. In this case, the leading edge became the people we know today as Apache.

The Name "Apache" is actually an Osage word for "Enemy" and wasn't even recognizable to these people or the Navajos. It was simply that the guides most often used by explorers into this region happened to be Osage, that this name was applied to these people.

The Apache

The Apache show the effects of a composite population, as they have a great deal of variation in height and shape as well as facial features.

By assimilating other peoples the Apache grew in number and had a sort of hybrid vigor. While this assimilation may at times have been considered slavery, the prospect of a under class of multigenerational workers was of no use in a hunter gatherer society.

So while the Apache did take captives it was done in order to assimilate them into their society not for creating a class of working slaves.

This was true to a lesser extent in their parent population the Navajo. Even after the introduction of sheep and an even greater dependence on agriculture the Navajo did not have a class of slaves.

Even the offer of horses for slaves was not enough to get the Apache or Navajo to round up other Indians and sell them to the Mexicans. Instead all the horses owned by the Apache and Navajo were the product of raids or purchases but not from the sale of slaves.

The Navajo

First contact for the Navajo with the Spanish came in 1571. By 1630 the Spanish were in a conflict with the Navajo and some Navajo were taken as slaves. By 1639 a force of 40 Spaniards and 800 allies invaded the land of the Navajo taking Navajo as slaves in a series of battles. After a brief period of peace while the Spanish used African Slaves, the Spanish again invaded the Navajos and attacked the Navajo at Acoma in 1669. After defeating the Navajo in the battle the Spanish began a series of slave gathering raids.

In 1698 the Navajo alerted the Pueblo and Apache tribes that a force of Spanish was invading. The Battles continued until 1698 with the Spanish more or less in control.

Mexico's war for independence from 1810 to 1821 set up a new neighbor for the Navajo. At a meeting with the Mexicans in Jemez Pueblo for a treaty in 1822, the Mexicans murdered the Navajo leaders and grabbed up as many Navajo for slaves as they could.

The Mexican American War brought the territory under American control by 1846. The civilian's continued to raid the Navajo for slaves and every effort by the Navajo to get their people back was seen as a "Hostile Indian attack" for which the US Army was supposed to respond.

By 1860 Mexican-Americans, Zuni and Utes were raiding the Navajo for slaves as well.

With the beginning of the American Civil War Union Troops were pulled out of the area to fight in the East, this left the Civilians unprotected, and in conventions held in Mesilla and Tucson in March of 1861 they voted to join the Confederacy.

In 1862 the Confederates under General Henry Hopkins invaded New Mexico. By March 2, 1862 the Confederates took Albuquerque New Mexico and by March 13th had taken the Capitol of Santa Fe. The Union tried a counter attack and were defeated by the Confederates at Glorieta Pass on March the 28th 1862. The Confederates then defeated another Union advance but the Confederate supply train was destroyed by fire forcing them to fall back.

Only a huge Union force arriving from California halted the Confederate progress. The Confederates would hold on to much of the area, including Arizona, until September 1863.

The Union New Mexico Militia in 1863, instead of fighting the Confederates, started raiding the Navajo taking slaves and stirring up another war with the Navajo. If this war was to end slavery you couldn't have guessed it from their actions.

In June 1863 Union General Carleton ordered 18 Navajo chiefs to surrender and that all their people were to come in to Fort Sumner New Mexico by July 20,1863. By September 1863 General Carleton ordered Colonel Kit Carson to defeat the Navajo. Col. Carson did a version of General Sherman's "March to the Sea" by invading the Navajo's Canyon de Chelly and destroyed the Navajo's fruit trees, crops and sheep. By January 1864 starving Navajo began to come in to Fort Sumner.

The Navajo Chief Manuelito surrendered in1866 and the last of the Navajo made the "Long Walk" to Fort Sumner. The Union Army had little enough for its own men let alone all these people. In the human tragedy that was happening at Fort Sumner General Carleton didn't know what to do. At the urging of the New Mexican ranchos Kit Carson was asked to offer the Navajo to be sold for slaves to willing buyers, Carleton considered the offer for some time but finally decided not to. Durring this period many Navajo children were taken as slaves. Even after the Navajo were allowed to return to a small portion of their old lands, the New Mexican civilians would take Navajo for slaves until 1886 and legally own them until 1911.

The Ute

The Ute were also primarily a hunter gatherer society and as such they could not see any use for a subclass of slaves. However despite their distrust of the Spanish the Ute were motivated to begin gathering people from all over the Great Basin and trading them for horses in New Mexico and Chihuahua. The Outlaw Trail as it was called went from Canada to Mexico and was made famous by the Outlaws Butch Cassidy and The Sundance Kid. The trail had been used for only a few years earlier by the Ute to haul Indian slaves South to Mexico. The area along US 50 at Corral reef has a bronze plaque commemorating the crossing of this trail at that point and states that an estimated five thousand or more Indian slaves were taken into Mexico along this trail alone.

The desire to get horses was an incredible motivation for the Ute as well as the Paiute and many tribes, who could see their standard of living improved by these animals.   The largest and most daring horse raid in the history of the West was made by the Ute. Chief Walkara of the Ute made a deal with Tomas Peg-Leg Smith, Phil Thompson, Levin Mitchell and my Great great grandfather, Bill Williams the Mountain Man. They had scoped out the huge horse herds located on the Catholic Missions at San Luis Obispo and San Juan Capistrano. The Church had taken many Indians as slaves to build and run these missions and they were more than willing to inform this enterprising group as to just where the Don's kept their prized horseflesh. The Utes, Peg Leg, Phil , Levin and my kin Bill managed to round up more than 3,000 of the best horses and drove them over Cajon Pass into the Mojave Desert. The Old Spanish Trail led from Los Angeles to Santa Fe New Mexico.

The Spanish were upset about their horses and a group of the Don's finest took up the trail. As the pursuing party came to a spring in the Mojave Desert. They dismounted and took a siesta as it was midday and fairly warm. In the tules near by were several Ute Warriors and my G-G-Grandfather Bill Williams. Dressed as Vaqueros they slipped, out of the tules and mounted the pursuing Mexicans horses, which they then rode off with. The Mexicans were cussing at them but were forced to walk back over the pass in their fancy riding boots. Some of the Mission Indians left with the Utes and Peg-Leg while others simply went back to their homes.

The Spanish Empire in Mexico

When the Conquistadores defeated the Aztecs it was only the beginning of a terrible set of events for the native peoples living in the Western Hemisphere.

The gold reserves of the Aztec Empire clearly showed that the metal was present in the New World. The demand for more gold required mining.

As the native population of Indians declined from the introduction of European diseases, the Spanish Empire looked to increase production by importing black slaves from Africa. These slaves could be easily identified from the general population, so if they ran away they could be easily located and recovered. The African slaves had two additional advantages over Indian slaves. First, they were less vulnerable to European diseases since their population had been in contact with these diseases for millennia, so they had immunity the Indians didn't possess; the other advantage was that the African slaves were not from the North American continent and would not have family or tribal members to assist them if they escaped.

Then there was the cost of the alternative! What would the Spanish have to pay Indians to bring other Indians to them as slaves? The Native population was already self-sufficient and such novelties as knives, glass beads, or liquor would only buy so much. To get slaves the Spanish would have to sell horses and large knives or weapons which could be used against them in the future; with this scenario the use of African slaves was the preferred option. The shift of control from Spanish to Mexican authority changed nothing. They continued to import male African slaves for mining operations.

The British declared slavery illegal in their possessions and began an international effort to end slavery or at least the acquisition of peoples into slavery. As early as 1808 the British, began establishing Naval bases along the West African Coast to initiate antislavery patrols. By 1827 the British operating from their naval base in Sierra Leon at Freetown, began to finally destroy the Cuban and Brazilian slave industry. The Royal Navy destroyed the last several forts, and all but three ships of the Cuban slave operation in 1828, thus putting them out of business.

The effect of this in Mexico was that Mexican Presidente Guerrero signed a decree in 1829 outlawing the importation of African slaves, abolishing slavery as such for Africans in Mexico; however, the Presidente was amenable with all sorts of Peonage which was even more brutal in many ways. This situation led to the need for Indian slaves to operate the Mexican gold, silver and quicksilver (mercury) mines. In order to get Indians to bring in Indian slaves, the Mexicans were willing to trade horses; this was the motivation for the increase in horse trading at this time.

For the Ute the horse took them from meager subsistence to lords of the Great Basin. Their subdivisions known to us as Paiute found the horse equally valuable and the slave trade kicked into high gear. Thousands of Indians were captured and marched across the Great Basin to buyers in New Mexico and Chihuahua.

In 1865 a recorded 3,000 Indians were processed as slaves in New Mexico, alone. The primary processing center was Cibolleta, near Pueblo of Laguna. There Indian slaves could bring as high as $500 a piece in 1875. This was ten years after the American Civil outlawed African slavery!! The primary source of these slaves were Navajo who were still being kidnapped into slavery in 1885. New Mexico did not outlaw this as "Peonage" until 1911.The Mexican state of Sonora continued slavery until 1939.

Sonora had a large Yaqui (Hiaki) population, who had benefited from agriculture and education provided by Jesuit Missionaries who were not in a position (or possibly inclined) to take the Yaqui as

slaves. In the 1730's the Spanish ordered the Jesuits to leave. The Franciscan Priests never got the respect of Yaqui, who then began to resent the "over lordship" of the Spanish. A Yaqui Leader named Juan Banderas in 1820 had the idea that the Yaqui, Mayo, Opata, and Pima tribes should unite and form their own republic separate from that of the new nation of Mexico. With the creation of the Mexican State, the Yaqui had been ordered to pay very high taxes to the state which the lands of Sonora, with their agricultural practices, could never afford. This was done in order to start a war with the Yaqui which the Mexicans believed they could easily win. When the Yaqui didn't provide the entire tax required, a Mexican Army was sent to force the Yaqui to do so. To the surprise of the Mexicans, the Yaqui were able to mount a successful Army of their own and drove the Mexican Army out, under the leadership of their leader Juan Banderas.

It wasn't until Juan Banderas was killed in 1833 that Mexico could start forcing the Yaqui off their lands and start taking large numbers into slavery for working mines and on Mexican-operated Ranchos.

The Mexican authorities continued to take Yaqui as slaves and brutalize them. In 1868 the Mexican army put 150 plus Yaqui in a church and set fire to it, killing all of them. This act brought another Yaqui leader named Cajeme to the front. He led a very successful war against the Mexican Army but by 1880 an outbreak of smallpox decimated the Yaqui and they were defeated again by the Mexican Army.

Presidente Porfirio Diaz' policy of ethnic transfer was enforced. More than 10,000 Yaqui and other Indians were enslaved and taken in chains to the Yucatan peninsula to work. Others were sold to Caribbean islands and thousands more to Bolivia, where they were enslaved working in the mines. Many Yaqui fled to the United States to escape this persecution.

This Mexican War on the Yaqui would not end until 1939. In 1971 my parents went down to the Mexican State of Sonora where my father had a friend who was engineering a hydroelectric project along the Rio Sonora for the Mexican Government. Dad's friend had married a Yaqui/ Terahumara woman and had a family. Men the same age as my father had rather visible scars from attacks by Mexican troops (on their villages) as children.

My neighbor, Ben Carrillo, is a result of this policy. Ben's Great Grandfather was a Mayo Chief in Sonora. He witnessed the destruction of Mayo Villages and wholesale enslavement of Indians.

This state of war against the Yaqui promoted a situation where the Mexican Army was in a position to take and process Indians for slavery.

The Mexican Army was supposed to clear hostile and or non-Catholic Indians from the land to make room for economic growth.

Since many Yaqui were nominally

A Mayo's Journey

by Benjamin Atojino-Carrillo

There are two dates in our family history that my father made sure I remembered, 1880 and 1910. My great-grandfather Atojino was a major Chief of the Mayo Indians. My great-grandmother Teresa, wife #4, was a captive from a raid on a wagon train and definitely not a Mayo Indian.

The Mayo are desert Indians from the State of Sonora in Northern Mexico, about 270 miles south of Arizona on the Mainland side of the Gulf Of California, Their lifestyle was very similar to the Yaqui, Apache and other Sonoran Desert tribes,

In 1880 something went wrong and a lot of Mayos died. My father told me Atojino my Great-Grandfather, felt the situation was hopeless. Atojino then took all five wives and about 30 children, and moved to the city (probably Navajoa). Once he got his large family to Navajoa he looked for a job.

He heard there was work at a bakery so he went to the back door of the bakery and knocked on the door. The owner of the bakery answered and asked what he wanted, he replied that he wanted a job. The owner asked him what his name was and he replied "Atojino". The owner said you can't have a name like that, you have to have a Spanish name. Written on a building next to the bakery was the name Carrillo, Atojino pointed to the sign and said "That's my name", and that is where our family name comes from, at least he didn't point at the outhouse.

I never understood what "went wrong" in 1880 that would cause a major chief to abandon his people and his culture. It wasn't until 2011 that the problems faced by my ancestors came into focus. I read my neighbor Guy Nixon's book, "Slavery in the West" and realized the magnitude of the disaster they faced. The alliance between the Mayo, Yaqui and Opata had, under their leader Cajeme, kept the Mexican army at bay for years. Cajeme's death and a major smallpox epidemic, probably orchestrated by the Mexican Army, so weakened their people that the Mexican Army was able to move into their homelands and enslave thousands of Indians.

Terahumara

I now realize that Atojino was terrified at the prospect of returning from a hunt to find all five wives and thirty children gone, and there would have been nothing he could do about it.

Atojino was an intelligent man and realized his only option was to try to move into a city where his family would be safe from slave raids and attacks by the Mexican Army or "Bestia".

After several years Atojino owned three bakeries, but he had five wives. My grandfather Fernando was from wife #4, that made him low man on the totem pole. Fernando felt he was smarter and worked harder than his brothers and deserved one of the bakeries. When Atojino told him that he would not get one of the bakeries, Fernando and his brother Arturo decided to cross the Sierra Madre Occidental into the Mexican State of Chihuahua to start their own bakeries. After several years they had established at least six bakeries in the area of Chihuahua City. Arturo had to take daily trips to his rural bakeries to bring supplies and collect money. As there were bandits in the rural areas he had to change his route frequently and protect himself. To do this he had bought a gun and was usually riding his horse alone between bakeries. However being Indian both Arturo and Fernando wore their hair long.

In 1910 the Mexican Revolution exploded into Northern Mexico. To counter this the central Mexican Government, under Carranza, passed new gun control laws which made the carrying of guns illegal. While Arturo was aware of this new law he had to carry money and with all the bandits he needed a gun for protection. He was traveling in a rural area when a unit of Federal Troops approached him and with nothing to hide he rode up to them; however, as he was obviously an Indian and was carrying a gun, they arrested him. He was executed the next morning, before Fernando even knew he had been arrested or had time to bribe the Federalies.

One of the counter forces to Carranza's Federalies was Poncho Villa. Poncho Villa was a Mestisto (part Indian and part Spanish) and had grown up with Mexican Government officials being legally allowed to rape his family members. Even with little education Poncho Villa had become successful and had been a businessman and mine owner in Sonora and New Mexico before the revolution. As such he had a vested interest in the country and raised his own army to counter Carranza's men.

Terahumara

Poncho Villa had not been able to get the local Indians to join him in Chihuahua and used this incident with Arturo to talk Fernando into recruiting Indians for him. Poncho explained what he would do for the Indians and what changes he would make if he won. Fernando saw Villa as a man who might help the Indians and was able to get several hundred Indians to join Villa's Army.

The family stories even have Poncho Villa having dinner with Fernando and our family and sleeping in our house.

Fernando's last day in Mexico started with Villa in his house and Carranza's Army under General Ocon approaching Chihuahua City. Villa decided to pull out leaving Fernando and his family. With his businesses in Chihuahua City Fernando decided not to pack up and leave with Villa's Army. As General Ocon took over Chihuahua City he grabbed Fernando's wife and children, game over. He then approached Fernando at his house and told him "Fernando we have a problem!, I have to kill twenty people in this city and you are number one on my list, don't worry about your wife and children I already have them."

Mexican General Obregon with Yaqui Staff

General Ocon let Fernando escape to El Paso on the train and them blew off the head of the town drunk, so he would have his twenty fresh bodies, for Carranza's inspector coming up from Mexico City, to see. Many years later General Ocon, who was by then also a refugee, spent a little time at Fernando's home in the United States. Also there is no story of Fernando paying off General Ocon with a bribe for his life, so I think Ocon realized Fernando was not really his enemy and took pity on him that day.

My Grandmother Beatrice, the true hero in our family, was held for awhile by General Ocon to make sure Fernando had left the country. If the inspector had arrived in Chihuahua City and seen Fernando it would have been General Ocon standing up against a wall being shot.

Beatrice and the children were taken with Ocon's army into the desert. As General Ocon's army had to move they began to discard some of their less valuable prisoners.

Beatrice and her three children were dropped off with a band of Indians the army came across in the desert. As there were numerous patrols roaming the country who might recognize her and the kids, they had to darken their skin with red clay to blend in with these Indians and avoid detection. Beatrice would not see her husband for a year and a half. Fernando made it to Juarez and then El Paso Texas. He got a job in a bakery and proved himself so well that he soon married the baker's daughter.

Beatrice knew that if Fernando had survived he would go to El Paso and she was determined to find him. Being a ?widow? with three children in a revolution wracked country, even if she found out that Fernando had been killed, she was determined to escape to the United States, she would make the two hundred mile journey across the Chihuahuan Desert, avoiding patrols and staying off the roads to Juarez. She checked bakery after bakery in El Paso and finally found Fernando with his new wife who was already pregnant.

Beatrice made an incredible achievement getting out of Mexico with three children, Jose, Beatrice, and Jenny, under conditions you can only imagine. How did she do it? Had the Carranza forces found her and the children they would have made an example out of them and if they survived they would probably have been sold as slaves.

Fernando and both of his wives raised a rather large family in El Paso operating and building bakeries. Five years after arriving in El Paso Beatrice gave birth to my father, Benino Jesus Carrillo a true Christian Gentelman, knighted by Cardinal Mc Intyre.

While this is my families story, I feel it is a typical survival saga representative of the horrors suffered by hundreds of thousands of Native American families due to slavery in the West.

Catholic they were often used by the Mexican Army as scouts to get other Yaqui and Mayo tribesmen, who were either hostile (if they were Catholic) or non-Catholic.

Under Presidente Porfiro Diaz the "Rurales" were organized and were given the "Ley Fuga" (Law of Flight) where they were allowed to shoot anyone who tried to run away. He intended to have a new prosperity by opening up the Northern part of Mexico to mining and ranching with permits paid by Mexican, European and American investors.

The town of Nuri in the Mexican State of Sonora became a processing center for Indian slaves brought down from the North. People from the Havasupai, Maricopa, Papago, Tohono O'odham and Chemehuevi were captured in the Arizona territory and brought down to Nuri to be processed as slaves.

The Catholic church owned many silver mines in Sonora and the yield from these mines was the primary source of income to the Catholic Church in Rome from Mexico. As it was considered immoral to enslave people with souls, the church elites debated whether Indians actually possessed souls. While the priests, who actually worked with the Indians, were convinced that the Indians DID have souls their superiors said that it was debatable.

The church established classifications of people based on skin color. In the church records for people you will find the following classifications. Espanol (for White,) Mestiso (for a person of half and half,) Indio (for Indian who was a catholic,) coyote (for an Indian who was dark skinned and not catholic) and Lobo (for the most undesirable) often referring to an Apache Indian.

Just South of Nuri were two major silver mines. One was owned by the church and the other by a coalition of powerful Dons. There were also many mercury mines, with shafts over 500 feet deep, operating in the Western foothills of the Sierra Madre.

Scouts U. S. Army

The life-expectancy for silver mine workers was only four years. The church was concerned that they were running out of labor and had passed an ordinance that expected every Indio family to have at least four children. The men were required to work 14 hour shifts at the church-owned mine.

The reality was that the Indios were dying-off and the supply of male Indios from the North was not compensating for these losses. To increase the number of new Indio slaves from the North, Colonel Luiz Gomez of Nuri sent out a decree to any banditos that they could be awarded immunity from former crimes if they would join the Mexican forces as "Bestia". They would not have to fight under the command of Mexican officers, but instead would be under their own command just as long as they did not commit crimes against towns and operations that were run by the church

Geronimo and fellow Apache photographed in the Sierra Madre of Sonora, Mexico

or the Dons. They would be supplied uniforms but would only get paid if they brought in Indians for slave labor.

Colonel Luiz Gomez soon found that he needed to make an additional requirement. In order to be paid for female Indios they had to have their reproductive organs intact. They would be paid more if the female indios had not been raped, but if raped they would receive almost no money if they were damaged to such an extent that they might have difficulty bearing children.

The Mexican Army at Nuri would pay 200 pesos per male Indio if he was healthy and able to work; less, depending on his condition. Female indios would bring about 100 pesos (or less) depending on their condition.

The male Indios were immediately sent South to the mines where the Army received 325 (or more) pesos apiece. If they were taken further South they might go for as much as 600 to 1000 pesos each, a profit of between 125 to 800 pesos per slave.

The female Indios of reproductive age were cleaned and inspected by the Army doctor then kept in a barracks inside the fort at Nuri. Here they were raped by the Mexican soldiers, who were under orders not to use any more force than was absolutely necessary. Once the female Indios were showing pregnancy they were shipped South, where they were sold for just as much as the male Indios, as the buyers expected to shortly have two slaves for their investment.

The sickly or older indios were sent to the mercury mines where an exposure of four days was lethal, the children were sold as house servants.

To better appreciate just how much of this occurred take these facts into account. During all the time that the area of Mexico could use African slave-labor, they only imported male African slaves. These slaves were so consumed in the mines that today's population of Mexico has less than one-tenth-of-a-percent that have any African genetics in them. The percentage of mixed-blood people having European and Indian blood accounts for more than 70% of the population of Mexico today. This is with pure-blood Indians still out-

147

numbering pure-blood Europeans twenty-five-to-one in Mexico. These are the results from slavery in Mexico.

The Apache were extremely difficult as they would not submit to slavery and were very likely to escape. To counter this all Apaches were branded with the letter A. The males were shipped in shackles immediately to the mercury mines, where with enough alcohol (and being kept in shackles) they were profitable. The female Apaches were shackled directly and shipped far to the South as soon as possible, where they brought a reasonable price.

One of the battles attributed to Geronimo, but not confirmed, was against the installation at Nuri. Geronimo and two other men dressed up as Bestia, with captured uniforms and hats, they led a group of Apache women who appeared to be chained together. They approached Nuri and asked (in Spanish) if the Colonel was in as they had a good catch. They were allowed to enter the gates of Nuri and when Colonel Luiz Gomez came out to view the merchandise, it is believed Geronimo was the one who drew out a revolver and shot the Colonel in the chest. The Apache women then dropped their chains and pulled out carbines that had been tied beneath their dresses. The Apache then killed all the Mexican soldiers and civilians they could, rescued those Indios in the facility, and set fire to it.

Several Mexican civilians did manage to get away. (It is with this more complete understanding of the situation that people can appreciate why surrendering to the Mexican Army was not a viable option for the Apache.)

Carmela as she walked into the Mexican Village

One little known fact is that the Chiricahua Apache did not all come in with Geronimo in 1886. While the surrender made an end as far as General Miles career needed it to be; In point of fact, the Chiricahua continued to live in the Sierra Madre long after this. In a court case determining land claims in May 13, 1950 Asa Daklugie (an Ndendaii Chiricahua) stated that not all of the Chiricahua came in with Geronimo. The rest of the

Chiricahua led by Chief Naiche's nephew Satsinistu, continued to live in the Sierra Madre. Apache were living "under the radar" so to speak through to the 1920's, before they began to conflict with the Mexicans of Sonora. In a final battle (in 1932) with Mexican Vaqueros several Apaches were killed, including a beautiful women with blue eyes which haunted the Mexican Vaquero who regretted the battle. In the weeks after that battle, several Apache children showed up in neighboring Mexican towns. One of the apache children was later named Julio Medina, and kept in Sonora Mexico, as he was considered able to do some work for the Mexican rancher. The other (who lived) was a little girl called Carmela.

The local Mexicans did not want Carmela as they still considered any Apache a problem, but an American couple on vacation were interested in adopting her. The Mexicans gave little Carmela to the American couple who returned to Los Angeles California where they formally adopted her. Carmela would graduate from L.A. High School in 1948. She later married a WWII veteran US Marine who was a White Mountain Apache. They lived and had a family on the White Mountain Apache Reservation.

General Miles needed a victory and an end to the Apache "Problem" for political reasons. The Apache's problems continued for another fifty years.

Now you know how the Apache Wars actually ended.

Carmela's High School Graduation

Photo from L.A. High School.

The Long History of Apache Slavery, the Genizaros of New Mexico and the Old Southwest.

Few realize just how long the Apache were taken as slaves. Due to the power struggle between the French and Spanish colonies, the tribes living in the border areas of these colonies were pressured to form alliances with the colonial powers. With the arrival of the horse the Comanche had given up their culture of sedentary villages based on the cultivation of corn in favor of the nomadic lifestyle of hunting buffalo.

This change in lifestyle was not entirely voluntary on their part. The effects of the eruptions of Indonesian volcanoes were disrupting agriculture all across the Northern hemisphere. From Poland to Connecticut there were years like 1814 when the crops completely failed and almost the entire population was forced to emigrate. As an exam-

Pictured above a Cherokee Woman

ple of this climatic volatility in New Hampshire on the 12th of July 1814 birds fell frozen to death from the sky and ponds froze over in August. For my ancestors the Osage Tribe living in Missouri, Kansas and Arkansas these weather variables were also recorded. My grandfathers grandfather was eight years old in 1851 when the summer temperature at the Osage Mission School, where he attended, reached 115 degrees as recorded by Father Schoenmaker's thermometer. Crops as well as people and livestock died en-mass across the entire region. White settlers from as far East as Herman Missouri, including many recently arrived German and Polish families, who had fled Europe due to these crop failures, agreed to take care of Osage homes, cattle and livestock while the Osage went on a massive fall buffalo hunt in the hope that the Osage would return with enough dried buffalo meat to keep them from starvation. In point of fact the Osage did manage to get enough buffalo on that fall buffalo hunt of 1851 to save not only themselves but the white families as well. These volcanic eruptions were making agriculture a very uncertain life style while hunting buffalo from horseback was now dependable.

Few if any historians have realized that these volcanic eruptions not only caused massive population displacement in Europe, resulting in European immigration to North America, but also caused the shift in the economies of the Native Americans as well.

As the Comanche were among the first to acquire the horse they soon became the dominant native power in the Southern Plains. They were so feared by the Spanish that they were soon being bribed with European goods and corn not to attack the various Spanish colonies. At the same time the French believed that a powerful alliance with the Comanche would protect their traders working in the Western areas of their colony of Louisiana.

The power of the Comanche and to a lesser extent the Wachita was soon being courted by both the French and Spanish. As the trade increased, the power of the Comanche also increased.

Pictured above an Osage girl sitting on a boulder along the Salt Fork of the Arkansas River.

In their efforts to expand the area of "Comancheria" the Comanche were now attacking other tribes. The practice of taking captives was commonplace and had been done by the Comanche even when they were agriculturally based. The captives were typically adopted into the tribe, ransomed back to their tribe or sold to other tribes.

The Frenchmen who were exploring and developing the French colony of Louisiana did not bring French women with them. Many tribes living along the Mississippi and other rivers encouraged their widows and surplus women to marry the Frenchmen. This encouraged friendship and trade but as the number of Frenchmen increased the demand for women soon exceeded the supply. As more and more French and Metis men came into the region to work the problem grew worse. The Comanche now found that they had willing buyers for young female captives. The tribe closest to the Comanche from which to take these captives (slaves) were the Lipan Apache.

AH-Weh-Eyu (Pretty Flower) a Senecah woman

While members of other tribes were taken as well namely some Pawnee, Navajo and Ute, the vast majority were Lipan and Kiowa Apache. These young women were purchased from the Comanche and soon became the wives of the French and Metis men.

In communities like Nacogdoches, the families of Frenchmen and Apache women were the foundation of the entire settlement. As the importation of Apache women continued for generations a language peculiar to the region developed. A dialect of Apache and pidgin French developed that was spoken by women, while the men spoke French. This would continue as a strange gender specific dialect that was dominant for women in settlements from Taos to Nacogdoches and San Antonio to Santa Fe.

The Lipan Apache women were genetically often rather petite and customarily wore their hair long often to their waist or even knees in length, as such they were considered very desirable. Due to this some Lipan Apache women were sold as far east as the Carolinas. It was this historic trade in Apache women, due to their beauty, that the Buffalo soldiers of the US Army in the 1880's stationed in the Forts servicing the Apache reservations, many of whom were part Seminole themselves, would make comments as to which Apache girls they wanted to take for themselves as payment. On several noted occasions it was these comments made by Buffalo Soldiers about the Apache women that convinced the Apache that the US Army was not going to protect the Apache families and lead to whole bands jumping their reservation and going renegade rather than being as they thought enslaved. The importance of these comments was not realized by the Officers of the US Army. The majority of these Officers were left over from the Civil War, a large percentage were originally from Northeastern states and were unfamiliar with the history of the Southwest.

A Sioux bride in her wedding dress

While the Apache women sold to the French were slaves their children by French and Metis men were not slaves. Because they spoke a French dialect this population was often considered to be Cajun by the Americans who later moved into the region. In reality the vast majority of the so called "Texas Cajuns" are not actually Cajun at all. Their descendants make up nearly 35% of the population currently living in East Texas.

Starting in 1629 the sale of slaves became a major business. In the Spanish colony of New Mexico these slaves and their offspring were referred to by several names depending on their degree of Indian blood as Pueblos, Genizaros, Coyotes or Vecinos.

Unlike their French counterparts these people and their children were still slaves. They and their offspring were the legal property of their Masters. In several letters and reports from the period it was noted that these slaves had fewer rights and an even more miserable life than the Black slaves living in the Deep South. The Southern States had passed laws that required the slaves masters to adequately feed and care for their slaves including once the slave had achieved old age, a sort of retirement plan by which the master could be legally and financially prosecuted for turning out and not caring for their slave once they were to old too perform labor. In contrast the Genizaros of New Mexico were often cast out to die of starvation once they were to old to work. The Catholic Church needed Indios for work and few would come in voluntarily for hard labor in exchange for the salvation of their souls.

Because of this the Catholic Church was willing to pay for Indian slaves as it was necessary not only to build their missions and farm the land but also to work in the Church owned mines. The Catholic Church had perhaps a more difficult time collecting money in New Mexico than in other parts of the Spanish Empire. This was largely due to the fact that nearly all the original immigrants were "Diaspora", the Spanish Jews who during the First Spanish Inquisition had converted to Catholicism rather than be killed. Then in an effort to generate more revenue the Catholic Church of Spain decided to have a Second Inquisition and so decided that these former Jews had not truly converted. As these families were now being targeted yet again, they immigrated en-mass to this most remote part of the Spanish Empire. Once in New Mexico these refugee Jews integrated well with the local Indian tribes. Later immigrants from Spain were more or less want-to-be aristocracy who wanted to live in a state where the wealth was based on estates worked by peons much like their Spanish homeland. These new Spanish Immigrants began taking slaves in large quantities to work the land grants they had received from the King of Spain.

For these slaves Spanish rule was miserable but with Mexican Independence from Spain in 1821 it only got worse. It got so bad that in 1837 the Genizaros, Vecinos, Coyotes and Pueblos rebelled and killed all the Mexican troops in Santa Fe and then cut the head off the Mexican Governor Albino Perez.

 They then elected their own government and chose a Genizaro of Pawnee ancestry named Jose Angel Gonzales as their Governor. It should be noted that the Deaspora had joined these rebels as they had no love for either the King of Spain or the Catholic Church.

 With this set of circumstances it is easier to understand why the Catholic Church revenue was lower than most other parts of the Empire. To make up for this difference in revenue the Church needed their mines to be productive.

Pictured below a Vecino with his mules hauling supplies in New Mexico, by 1900 nearly 85% of the people living in New Mexico either were Genizaros or were descendants of them.

It is a stereotype of the Victorian Age that Native American Women were basically ugly and undesirable squaws. In point of fact the first American citizen to make prima Ballerina of Europe was Maria Tallchief (Pictured above) an Osage Indian born in the town of Hominy on the Osage Reservation. The Osage were forbidden to dance by the Federal Government and Bueru of Indian Affairs but Maria Tallchief and her sister danced anyway. Maria Tallchief becoming the first woman from the United States to achieve the position as Prima Ballerina of Europe. Not exactly what you were lead to believe watching television while growing up is it?

As Church profits would be much lower with hired workers they used Indian slaves instead.

It must be noted that many of the priests sent to this remote region were not exactly "First Stringers" and were not the best examples of the Catholic priesthood.

For those readers questioning this history I must recommend Estevan Rael-Galvez's Doctoral Dissertation titled Identifying Captivity and Capturing Identity American Indian Slavery in Colorado and New Mexico 1776-1934. His work gives the actual names and court cases of the Genizaros.

In one court case The parish priest Padre Martinez was charged with holding Indian captives. It was noted that the Padre had purchased a young Navajo girl who he later named Rosario. At the time of his trial Padre Martinez had two sons from Rosario and had two other Indian slaves in his possession.

Another court case charged two priests with purchasing and owning a number of slaves over a period of several decades. It seems that these two priests had purchased young Indian girls and later sold their offspring as slaves over a period of twenty or more years. Padres Gabriel Ussel,

A Kiowa Apache Girl

Ramon Medina and Mariano Lucero all of Taos were also convicted on similar charges.

In researching the available material it becomes obvious that this practice was very wide spread in the community at large as well. In another case Juan Benito Valdez was found to have owned at one time more than thirty Indian slaves. The children he sired were still slaves at the time of his death.

By 1890 nearly 85% of the people living in New Mexico were Genizaros or their descendents. While the slavery of Genizaros living in New Mexico was finally outlawed in 1911 it would remain legal in Mexico for two and a half decades more. The actions of the Apache during the this period make more sense once you realize the history of the Apache and the reality they would face if taken by the Mexicans.

Another new set of records and historical documents concerning this area and period of time have only recently become available.

Prior to the American Civil War President Buchanan had to fight another Civil War. Known as the Anglo– Mormon War or Buchanan's Blunder this war started when the ardent supporters of the Mormon Religion under the leadership of Brigham Young attempted to seceed from the United States and form their own country called Deseret. In addition by practicing polygamy the Mormons were breaking Federal law. The situation came into focus when the Mormon Militia surrounded and besieged a wagon train of American settlers from Arkansas. After agreeing to a surrender all the men and women as well as all but a handful of the children were then summarily executed.

The Mormon immigrants who went to Tres Rios enjoyed hunting but respected the resource
and did not waste it they were anti-slavery and did not drink or sell alcohol, as they could not
go back to the US they didn't want the US Army around but they didn't necessarily trust the
Mexican authorities either. This made them natural allies of the Apache. Only since 1995 have
the family papers and records of the Tres Rios Mormons become available, revealing the extensive trade and contact between them and the Apache.

The survivors being children considered to small to remember the incident who were adopted into Mormon families. The incident became
known as the Mountain Meadows Massacre.

As the news of this incident leaked out it became the final straw and
the US Army was dispatched under General Sydney Johnson to end the
"Mormon Uprising" at it was called in 1857-1858.

While the US Army did not in fact have to attack the Mormon Forces
before Brigham Young backed down there were a considerable number
of Mormon men who were wanted by the US Federal Government and
had warrants out for their arrest.

The prosecution of those Federal warrants was however put on hold
when the US Army was splintered by the eruption of the War Between
the States (American Civil War).

To avoid prosecution and prison or possibly death sentences in the
United States many of these Mormon Men and their families sought
refugee status in Mexico. At the end of the American Civil War with
the Federal victory it was only a matter of time before these Mormon
men would be arrested.   Seeing an opportunity for economic growth
Presidente Porifiro Diaz of Mexico granted the Mormons asylum in

Mexico. These Mormon Families were given a land grant in the Tres Rios region of Northern Sonora.

These Mormons were predominately polygamists but some were former members of the Mormon Militia who had participated in the Mountain Meadows Massacre, as such they all realized that they could not return to the United States, yet they had family ties and economic interests North of the border.

For the Apache these Mormons were an asset. The Mormons were largely converts from England which was staunchly anti-slavery, add

Pictured above and below a Yaqui/Apache in Sonora, who would be called a Genizaro or Coyote by the Catholic Church, working as a cowhand and hunting guide. The only protein for him or his family being wild game meat.

to this the fact the Mormon's did not allow alcohol. The Mormons were not keen to have the Mexican Military in or around their settlements but were also afraid of any US Army incursions into Mexico which might arrest them in the process.

While the Mormons enjoyed hunting they did not wantonly kill the wild big game animals and valued this resource. In addition they were always very respectful toward the Apache.

Because of this the Apache were soon trading heavily with the Mormons living in the Tres Rios country. The mutual enemies made them natural allies and they soon developed a strong trust for one another. The Mormons would sell the Apache the latest in modern American firearms while the Apache provided a level of security from both American Army Units and Mexican forces.

The Mormon's would prosper in Tres Rios until the Mexican Revolution when Mexican Federal Army commanders and Rebel Commanders alike considered the Mormon settlements an available resource base for their

armed forces to strip. By that time most of those Mormons who had warrants out for their arrest had died of old age, so the bulk of the Mormon
population living in Tres Rios fled North to the United States.

The mutual assistance between the Apache and Mormons was almost unknown until recently when the family diaries and letters of the Tres Rios
group were finally opened up to the public by the Mormon Church in their
efforts to become more mainstream and not viewed as a cult in the 1990's.

This history was initially brought to my attention as a youngster when my
father's friend Al Shand married a Yaqui/ Terahumara woman named
Nancy from Sonora. Dad's Friend convinced my father to come help him in
engineering a hydro-electric plant on the Rio Sonora just East of Merchichi
not far from Banamichi.

In the 1970's the Mexican government had worked out a deal with the
World Bank and was building hydroelectric and agricultural dams along the
major water courses of the country.   Dad's friend was one of the Engineers
who worked on the Ouiachic and Aguamilpa dams in Sonora Mexico.

My father, Mother and I went down to Merchichi and lived in a house in
this small town. The townspeople owned the land in slices like a pizza radi-
ating from the town center. The homes in Merchichi didn't have electricity
or running water and had dirt floors, but they were very clean and comfortable. They used a special clay for the floors which hardened to a smooth
shiny surface, the kerosene lamps provided the home with a comfortable
light and a few pitchers of water and a wash basin made it far from primitive.

My father was quick to came up with a way of using the conveyor to bring
the rock from the quarry down to the dam site that would use the generator
as a brake and generate electricity for the operation in the process. This and
other ideas were what my fathers friend wanted him for. My father did not
act like the typical Mexican Governmental engineer who usually saw themselves as being of a higher social status than the local residents and typically annoying the workers and residents alike.

By contrast my father worked with the locals and having grown up in a
rural area he was perhaps more familiar and comfortable with doing this. I
enjoyed playing with the kids, riding horses and going to their school. My
mother had a milk goat goat at our home and also having grown up on a
farm found they had a great deal in common. As such we blended in more
than stood out and the local people felt more comfortable around us than the
Mexican Engineers.

159

The Canyon Del Cobre in Mexico is just a magnificent as the Grand Canyon

I recall it was a rather hot afternoon and I was swimming near the job site. It was probably a surprise to the local men when my father stripped down to his underwear and joined me in the creek. The men quickly followed his lead and soon they were all in the creek. It was now that I and my father noticed that many of the men my fathers age and older were often covered in scars while the younger men didn't have any scars.

In asking these men why the older ones had scars and the younger ones didn't we learned that the Mexican/ Yaqui War hadn't ended until 1940. My father born in 1931 was the same age as many of these men, who in their youth were mostly wounded by artillery fire in the last battles of this war.

From the turn of the 19th century well into the 20th century the primary buyer of Mexican crude oil was Germany. Adolph Hitler even requested permission to build a German Naval Base at Vera Cruz but the request was denied by the Mexican government. Because of this the Mexican Army was being equipped with the latest in Krup field artillery complete with German military advisors on how to use it. Prior to the arrival of this artillery the Yaqui with their sentries posted could typically evacuate their villages before the Mexican soldiers or cavalry could open fire on them. With the German advisors the Mexican Army could with out any warning shell Yaqui villages from miles away. The scars we saw on these men were from these attacks.

These communities were a mixture of Yaqui with refugee Apache, Mayo and Terahumara mixed in. We learned from them that even after the war ended the Mexican Government was still hostile toward then and as recently a 1955 the Cortines Decree had stripped the Yaqui of their water rights.

On his time off my father took us on trips around the area. Often the locals wanted to show us interesting places and wildlife. Dad took us North and saw the Mormon Towns built of pine lumber the same as my grandparents home and we took the train through the Canyon del Cobre and Barranca del Cobre which were much like our Grand Canyon all the way to Topolobampo.

I enjoyed the people, country and have good memories of this experience and it has affected my outlook to this day.

Crow Indian woman by a stream

My fathers work took us into the very heart of the Sierra Madre where Geronimo, Nachie and the Chericowa Apache had lived. Some of the men we met had Apache ancestry as their ancestors had escaped to join up with the Yaqui people in Sonora. Pictured above Gerinimo and the Chief Niche in 1880. It is an interesting note that Cochise had taken a Baca Girl as a wife even though two of his other Apache wives objected. Because of their objections Cochise had to by custom fight two of his brothers-in-law to the death in order for the offspring of his Baca wfie to be recognized by tribal custom. It was from this wife of Cochise that Niche descended. Because Jewish custom says that the children of a Jewish woman are jewish as well, to many of the old Jewish families of New Mexico Chief Niche was part of their extended family as well as blood kin. For the US Army who was not aware of this family connection it seemed very peculiar when some New Mexicans would go out of their way to assist the Apache.

Shoshone Mike and the Last Indian Battle of The United States

We tend to believe that the last battle fought against the Native Americans was the Battle of Wounded Knee, against the Sioux, but that is not true. The last battle was fought in Northern Nevada in 1911 and it was the result of white men trying to enslave Indians.

This story is a bit personal for my Father. My Father went to college at the University of Nevada Reno and many of his friends were from families who lived in Northern Nevada. Dad would take his Model T Ford all over the area from Reno to Idaho and Oregon.

My Father did not travel on the major roads, as a matter of fact he and his Model T often traveled the still-clearly-visible wagon trails. Dad always was a history buff and he often tried to follow copies of maps made by the first explorers of the region.

Durring his travels he would stop and visit the families of his college and Navy friends who lived in this country, as well as the Shepherd's and Indians he came across. Unlike most men in his generation, Father would take the time to listen to the old timers' stories, and due to his own Indian heritage he listened just as intently to the Indians stories and their point of view.

As a young man my   Father went into this vast expanse in his Model T Ford.

This vehicle was recognized by the locals and enabled him to get into many ranches and reservations he probably would not have otherwise been able to visit.

My Father and his Model T Ford in the Black Rock Desert of Northern Nevada in the mid 1950's.

Later, my Father would take me into this country on many trips, both with his work and to visit the awesome places and people he knew. Many of these trips with me were in the same Model T Ford.

One story, that was often told to him and that I later also heard, was about the tale of Shoshone Mike. Every account added a few details but in researching the story, it was interesting that the Indians' account of the events was not included in the official stories. Here then is the compilation of all the accounts that both my Father and I have heard and read about this last battle of the Native Americans.

Shoshone Mike's actual name was Ondongarte, but he went by Mike Daggett. He was also called Salmon River Mike, Indian Mike and Rock Creek Mike. In 1910, Mike's family consisted of his wife; three teenage sons (one whose name I couldn't find) then Charlie and Gnat; two older daughters Snake (Isa) age 16 and Toad (Pia) several years older (Possibly not a daughter at all, but Gnat's wife); two adolescent sons the older one named Eat-em-up-Jim, the other one (aged 7) and four little children (one who was 4) and (one only 10 months old,) thirteen in all.

It is possible that these were all his children, but even the Indians said that it was possible that Toad was the wife of Mike's son Gnat, and that at least the 10 month old was Gnat and Snakes baby, who was later named Mary Jo Estep.

The family was living on the reservation near Fort Hall, Idaho. Here they were hard working successful farmers. In 1890, Mike and his family were forced off their farm by white settlers who claimed they had "purchased" the land. These settlers were backed up by the sheriff, who was (curiously) also the land agent in the area. Although Mike had been respected by the people in the area and his older children were attending school, they were not allowed to occupy any land in the area.

The Indian agent was completely useless and probably responsible for the problem. Mike and his family moved South into the arid un-occupied area of Northern Nevada and Northeastern California, and began to live more traditionally.

Mike and his sons took work on ranches in the Little Salmon River country in Northern Elko County. The ranchers remembered Mike and his family as very hard-working and honest, but tended to stay to themselves. Paiute in the area said that Mike and his family didn't socialize with them either and they believed by their accent, that Mike and his family were probably Bannock or Goshute , but could have been Shoshone. They believed that Mike claimed to be Shoshone because in school his children had read about Sacagawea and the Lewis and Clark Expedition. If the ranchers felt any Indian tribe was "Good" it was the Shoshone, so Mike claimed to be Shoshone, whether he was or not, and lived peacefully for twenty years.

The bodies of the three Basque Shepherds; John Laxague, Peter Erramouspe, Bertrand Indiano and the Cattleman; Harry Cambron loaded on sleds for removal from the High Rock Canyon in February 1911.

The ranchers knew them as well as the local Paiute but the family kept to themselves and lived in a more or less traditional way. In 1910 a known cattle -rustler named Frank Dropp, shot and killed one of Mike's older sons.   Enraged at the senseless murder of their brother Charlie and Gnat trailed Frank Dropp and killed him on Cow Creek in Elko County. Afraid of future problems Mike took the family South.

By the winter of 1910, they were camped in the Northeast end of the Black Rock Desert in the Little High Rock Canyon, which today is a four-hour-drive from Gerlach, or about 135 miles North of Reno Nevada. Mike and his family were having a hard time, as the sheep herders by killing and over grazing overgrazing, had decimated the wild game in the area. With all the worlds' armies wearing wool uniforms, the demand for wool was at an all time high as the events leading to WWI were starting to fall into place.

Facing the prospect of starvation, Mike had killed a couple of cattle, cutting the meat up and stored some by putting it in a tree to freeze.

Several Basque Shepherd's had come across Mike's family and talked to Mike. Mike (or one of his sons) had asked if they had any .25/35 rifle cartridges they could trade for, but the Basque didn't have that caliber of round. Mike had purchased a Winchester .25/35 rifle from a rancher several years before and this makes sense. The shepherds also noticed Isa and Pia, "Mike's daughter–in-law and 16 year old daughter. They made graphic gestures to see if the girls were interested in having sex with them. The girls and Mike's son told them to leave then and that they had worn out their welcome.

Mike was afraid that the shepherds might have smelled the beef cooking or seen the meat stored in the tree, but he figured that he could work it out with the cattlemen if they found out.

It was a day or two later, near the end of January 1911, when the three Basque shepherds, John Laxague, Peter Erramouspe, Bertrand Indiano with Harry Cambron (a cattleman) came riding into High Rock Canyon.

They rode up to the camp rather fast and surrounded Mikes camp. Harry Cambron said that they were guilty of rustling cattle and that they were going to get some value from them. Two of the Basque shepherds rushed up on Toad and grabbed her, one held her arms behind her back while the other began to tear her dress open. The other shepherd had a rope and was saying he should hang the old Chief Mike, at this time Shoshone Mike was estimated to be nearly seventy years old. The fact that these men had not told anyone else where they were going, and had brought only one gun (a pistol) with them indicated that they did't fear Mike and his family at all.

Harry Cambron and the Shepherds were talking about how much money they might get for Toad by selling her to a camp of Shepherds some distance to the West and also that they might get some money for the younger girl Snake. As two of the Shepherds were busy holding and tearing Toads dress apart, Harry Cambron and the other Shepherd were walking up to Mike with a rope. They did not notice Charlie and Eat-em-up-Jim, who had been out of camp when they had rode in. Charlie had the family shotgun while Eat-em-up-Jim had a bow and arrow.

Only the cattleman had a gun and it was a .44 caliber automatic. Charlie saw that only the cattleman was armed so he motioned to Eat-em-up-Jim to arrow the man beside their father. Charlie shot Harry Cambron with the shotgun in the back, as Eat-em-up-Jim arrowed Bertrand Indiano.

At the shot Harry fell instantly and Bertrand screamed. Peter, who was holding Toads arms let go and Toad lunged forward, knocking John down, (who had been tearing her dress apart). Toad grabbed the camp axe from beside the camp fire and turned with it in time to crush Peters face. Charley reloaded and now shot John in the chest. Then, as Bertrand tried to get to a

The Posse; Captain Donnelly and Charles Stone of the Nevada State Police, The Sheriff of Modoc County California Joe Reeder, and deputies George Holmes, Hennry Huges, Otto Van Oruan, William Parsons, Warren Prutt, Matt West, Ben Cambron, Ed Hogle, frank Perry, Charles Byrne, Merrill Pressea, and Jack Fergeson. Not pictured were the two Piute Trackers Skinny Pascal and unnamed tracker

horse Toad hit him in the back of the neck with the axe. Bertrand was still standing but Charlie had reloaded and now shot him in the head.

To note about Harry and the shepherds' actions: It was fairly common for Shepherds and cattlemen to ride down and grab young Indian women and girls. They were particularly vulnerable when gathering Pinyon nuts. Several women remembered being taken in this manner. One recounted that she was taken to the camp of two Basque Shepherd brothers who took turns watching her and raping her. It wasn't until many months later, with her pregnancy so far along that sex was becoming somewhat difficult, that the brothers let her leave to return to her family as best she could.

Another woman was taken and kept chained to a wagon when the shepherd wasn't around. She had three children by the shepherd until the shepherd didn't return for three days, which was very unusual. She managed to have her oldest child bring some tools that were always kept beyond the length of her chain, she cut the chain and took the three children with her, back to her people.

These stories were very common and many people who were a generation or two older than my father that lived in the area were the result of these kinds of actions. It was kept secret for the most part but around a campfire they sometimes explained why they had the name they had, and the story would come out.

Now, Mike and his family were scared.
They took the clothing of the dead men and
modified it to fit the little children. The
men's bodies were hidden in the willows
near the creek and the family left High
Rock Canyon. Mike took the family East
across the Black Rock Desert and over into
the Quinn River country.

It wasn't until February 10, 1911 that the
bodies of the four dead men were found in
the willows in High Rock Canyon. The
word got out that an "Indian Uprising" was
happening and that a band of renegades
were on the loose, headed by Shoshone
Mike. California and Nevada began to as-
semble a posse to track down the renegades.

Captain Donnelly and Charles Stone of
the Nevada State Police joined the Sheriff
of Modoc County California, Joe Reeder,
with the following deputies; George
Holmes, Henry Huges, Otto Van Orman,
William Parsons, Warren Prutt, Matt West,
Ben Cambron, Ed Hogle, Frank Perry,
Charles Byrne, Merrill Pressea, and Jack
Fergeson.

While no picture of Shoshone Mike alive
exists he was killed wearing a traditional
war bonnet as is being worn by Shoshone
Warrior Rabbit Tail pictured here.

The Nevada State Police hired two Paiute trackers who had worked for them
many times in the past and who knew Shoshone Mike. One Paiute tracker
named Skinny Pascal would later give testimony that was a bit counter to that of
the other deputies.

The posse went out to High Rock Canyon, where Skinny Pascal picked up the
over two week old trail of Mike and his family. The trail was old, but Skinny
was an expert, and for two hundred miles he tracked them, through the Black
Rock Desert across the Quin River Country and over the Santa Rosa Mountains,
then East toward the Little Humbolt River country. Finally on February 26,
1911 they caught up with Mike and his family at Kelly Creek, just North of
Golconda Nevada.

Mike and his family had seen the posse coming and began their death chant.
Pascal tried to call out to Mike, but the eager deputies began shooting.

Ed Hogle shot Shoshone Mike with one of the first shots, from nearly 150 yards away, and began shouting, "I've killed Mike, I've killed Mike"! Ed then began running toward Mike's body. When Ed got to within thirty feet, Mike raised up on his elbow and shot Ed with Harry Cambron's automatic .44 caliber pistol, killing Ed.

The posse took their time now but shot all of Mike's sons, and began to get closer. Mikes wife had Mary Jo Estep on a cradle board on her back. She had a spear and tried to get away.

Pia, stood up and began to sort of dance toward the posse swaying her hips from side to side. This caught the men by surprise and when she got to within thirty yards she fell down and Eat-em-up– Jim stood up and shot an arrow wounding one of the posse. The posse then mowed he and Pia down in a hail of bullets, Mikes wife was then observed and shot down as well.

The posse then rushed in and grabbed Isa, Mike's ten year old son, and a toddler. Upon inspection they found that Mary Jo Estep was still alive so they cut the ten month old baby from the cradle-board still attached to her dead mother's body.

The weather had been incredibly cold and the ground was frozen so a hole was made with dynamite, and the dead bodies of Mike and his family were thrown in.

The posse then went back to Reno where the baby (Mary Jo Estep,) Isa, the ten year old son and the toddler were locked up in the Reno jail for several months.

Shoshone Mikes war bonnet that was re-covered after the "Battle". It is now in the Nevada State Historical Museum located in Elko Nevada.

Isa was forced to confess the story about her family killing the white men and added that a Chinaman was also killed. The summer before a Chinaman had grabbed her and was trying to tie her up when Gnat found them and killed the Chinaman. However, part of her account was not written down according to the Indian translator who gave his recollection of the confession several weeks later.

A stockman dug up the bodies of Mike and his family and shipped them to the Smithsonian Museum. The site of the battle is now in the middle of a gold mine and has been dug up.

The surviving members of Shoshone Mikes family in front of the Reno Jail. Mary Jo Estep is the Baby in the arms of her sixteen year old sister Isa known as Snake.

Les Sweeney of Payette, Idaho, worked on the story of Shoshone Mike for twenty years and wrote a book about it titled "Only one Survived" written about Mary Jo Estep the baby of the family.

The wounds of this affair were still very fresh forty years later, when my Father was roaming Northern Nevada, and the story was still a topic of conversation around the campfire and in the remote ranch house.

To this day, the relatives of Shoshone Mike and other Indians in the area would like to see the story told honestly. This is what I have tried to do.

Conclusion

In looking at the entire history of slavery in North America I came to a few conclusions that I felt I should share with the reader.

First; the institution of slavery as practiced by Native Americans well before the coming of Columbus was not any different than what was practiced in the rest of the world. As the statistics point out the percentage of slaves for Alaska was identical to that of Sparta during the time of the Greek Republic. That some tribes practiced slavery while others did not, does not indicate that some had any higher moral standards than the others, it was determined by economics, nothing more nothing less.

Second; our current history only deals with the slaves of African decent, while records and genetics prove that a large percentage of slaves came from Ireland, while the enslaved Native Americans are completely omitted. The history taught in our schools relegates slavery to the Southern American States and has it ending in 1865, while in fact it lasted until 1911 and encompassed much of the lower 48 states as well as Alaska and continued in Mexico until 1936.

Third; I have found that the institution of slavery had a great deal to do with many of the wars fought against the Native Americans, yet I can not find a single Hollywood movie that even mentions this subject in the giant volume of Western films made.

Many Americans and a large number of students today are of the opinion that the United States Government's treatment of Native Americans was worse than that of Mexico, Central America or South America. I think the true and honest history no matter how blunt and shaded should be taught for the sake of humanity. The fact is the United States was no worse and in some ways a little better than most.

Finally, I would hope that the many minority groups who crave media exposure to forward their cause might admit that one minority took abuse far longer and to a greater degree than all the other minorities in America. That the original owners of America could be legally enslaved until 1911, that even after getting citizenship in 1927, many would not have the right to vote until 1948.

It is my hope that this book might stir some interest in this forgotten part of history.

The "Singing / Talking" Stones.

Japajto-oo/ Tittii-Tom-oo

It would be appropriate to go into a little more depth about this fascinating aspect of Maidu / Miwok technology. The majority of immigrants viewed the Native tribes as inferior both culturally and in intelligence.

Om-blu'-kai located just of the east side of Oak Hill Road a few hundred feet South of Squaw Hollow Creek is Archeological site #150.

To make the assumption that a people or society who are operating in the "Stone Age" are lacking intelligence is a gross miscalculation. As a matter of fact, by percentage of the population, a hunter gatherer society has a considerably higher level of intelligence compared to an agriculturally based society. The reason is rather simple. A hunter gatherer society does not have the "security net" provided by agriculture, so those individuals in a hunter gatherer society who made poor choices, were unproductive or not providing valuable services, simply were not sustainable and died.

As an aside, note that the First American fighter pilot to make an air to air combat kill and the first American to make Prima Ballerina of Europe, as well as many of America's leading scientists and engineers, were only one to three generations removed from-stone-age-based societies. In the thousands of years the Maidu and Miwok lived in California they were not technologically stagnate.

One of their more impressive feats was their integrated communications network. Referred to by various translations as "Singing Stones" or "Talking Rocks" these were actually communication receiving and transmitting stations, they are probably best thought of as "telegraph Stations". These stone formations were discovered by Maidu and Miwok scientists. By extraordinary experimentation and research they found those stone formations that were connected to other formations at considerable distance from one another could be used to communicate. The longest known and verified "Line" is 14 miles long. By explanation; this is to say that the distance between two "Singing Stones" located in El Dorado County is 14 miles where a tap on one is clearly audible on the other 14 miles away.

K-ocos-oo

The stone formations have qualities such that they are rather dense materials like granite, slate, or basalt. They must not have fractures or faults breaking their run from one point to another.

The principle is the same as taking two empty metal food cans and by attaching a string to the center of both can lids then stretching the cans apart so that the string is taught. The tap (or voice) in one can causes the lid "diaphragm" to vibrate which, by transmission down the string, causes the other lid to replicate the sound.

Depending on the material of which the stone formation is made, different frequencies were possible. By mechanically tapping a surface on the transmitting stone that was orientated to the "End Grain" of that stone, you could transmit a message. This is to say that you will not transmit a message on the can and string system by tapping the side of the can or string. Transmission is only possible by sending the pulse down the grain of the stone formation. The receiver had to position their ear at a right angle to a face on the stone that had end grain to be able to hear the transmitted sounds.

The Maidu and Miwok scientists were very aware of geology and the properties of various types of stone. They knew which types made the best tools, and how the grain of a stone affected their ability to work it into the tools essential for survival. The typical "Singing Stone" was manned by at least two "Listeners" and one or more runners.

The "listeners" (operators) were usually members of the society with vision or mobility issues who by doing this provided a valuable service to the society.

The transmissions were typically done in a code similar to our "Morse Code". Unfortunately this unique code has been lost. Those who heard it remembered that it consisted of reports followed by pauses. There are even some reported accounts where the transmission was made by the operator's

K-ocos-oo

Turtle Rock (K-ocos) Is located near the intersection of Hanks Exchange Road and No Walk Drive. Also referred to as Haranguer's Rock it is also a registered archeological site in El Dorado County. Like most of these sites they are located on private property and it would be deeply appreciated that the land owner's rights be respected as well as the rights of the Maidu and Miwok people whose culture these belong to.

voice. The operator didn't talk into the stone but made low protracted tones at various intervals that resonated. The receiver could hear these tones at the other end and translate the message. The Voice operated "Singing Stones" were typically very dense stone and the "transmission lines" were not longer than a mile or two.

The stations had to use runners to relay information from one station to the next and to the nearby villages. These "stations" were manned all day long, typically by persons with vision or mobility issues, who needed the surrounding area quiet to listen, these were taken as "pagan shrines" by the new immigrants. These new commers felt justified in trying to destroy these "stations", as they assumed they were altars to the devil or "Red Devils".

While we don't know the entire length of the system which was located here in

A (Titti-Tom-oo)

the Sierra Nevada, we do have an insight as to the speed with which messages could be transmitted when the system was in place and fully manned.

In 1844 Kit Carson and John C. Fremont were coming to California, when they came to present day Sly Park (Chu-Ni in Miwok Tgo-No in Maidu) the news of their arrival was put on the communication network. A Miwok man known as "Walker", born approximately in 1815, lived in Murphy's California. He had heard of Kit Carson and wanted to see this man. Walker had never seen a white man before, but was very interested to see this one in particular.

In the story related by Walker (around 1900) to a French miner-turned-farmer, named Marshal. Marshal who was a new immigrant, didn't know "Who, Kit Carson was", when the tale of this journey was related to him.

The grain of the stone's formation determines the place where a transmission can be made from as well as where to listen for incoming signals.

This site I was able to photograph but not give the name or location of.

Walker heard that Kit Carson had arrived in Chu-Ni and decided to go and look at this man. Walker made his way North and found Kit Carson and Fremont at the American River (wakalu tenoka Alleni-k). Walker saw Kit Carson, who was a surprise to him. He recounted that the man was much taller than most Miwok and when he shook Kit Carson's hand it was a very large hand. Walker left the meeting very impressed with Kit Carson but not as impressed with Fremont.

The speed of information can be extrapolated to some degree by this story. By measuring the distances the message traveled from Sly Park to Murphy's, then, to walk on foot from Murphy's to catch Kit Carson, on horseback; had traveled from Sly Park down to the American River (probably near Folsom). Indicates that the "communication network" was two and a half to three times or more faster than a man could walk.

There are "Talking Rocks" Japato-oo/ "Singing Stones" Tittii-Tom-oo, located throughout the Sierra Nevada that were part of the Maidu/ Miwok's Communication network.

Only a few individuals know of the locations of these unique sites and understandably are reluctant to tell. This "Japajto-oo" like many has lost its name but not it's significance.

Maidu and Miwok Foods

It would interest some readers to know what foods were available to the native people of the Sierra Nevada.

Meat, the most widely documented source for food, has little written about it and less understanding of how it was processed and preserved.

While a deer or grouse killed fresh might be cooked and eaten by the hunters, or if reasonably close enough to their village taken back, it doesn't explain how it was preserved or transported for longer distances.

Blacktail deer were the most common large animal

Many hunter kills were simply too distant from their families or villages to be taken back fresh enough for consumption. In California much of the year the temperature is too warm for meat to last outside for more than three to four days before it will rot and become inedible. This made processing of the meat absolutely necessary to save this valuable resource for later consumption.

An example of one of these processes comes down from my Grandfather's hunting experiences as a young man on the Osage Indian Reservation.

There were antelope on the Western part of the Indian Territory and it was about a week or so ride by horseback for Grandpa and several other boys to get there. In the group there was one double barreled muzzle loading shotgun and a cap and ball revolver, the rest of the boys had bows and arrows.

As recalled, the strategy was for the two boys with the guns to be dropped off in a depression where the natural features of the landscape would confine the antelope to run over that position. The others would then ride out and sort of herd the antelope so that they would be inclined to move over the position of the two with the guns. Once the antelope were close enough the two would shoot their guns and the others would ride down and arrow the cripples.

The antelope were then carefully gutted so as not to rupture the stomach. The stomach was then tied in a knot at the upper end. The entire stomach was pulled inside-out so that the inner lining was now on the outside. This was then placed in water.

The meat was cut into fairly small thin strips and placed in a copper bucket with water. Salt was added to the water and the meat stirred until the meat changed to a bluish color, this indicated that the meat was saturated with salt. The time required to do this depended on the temperature and the thickness of the meat pieces. These strips were then laid out on a piece of wire mesh which they had brought rolled-up, it was now unrolled over a hole they had dug. The meat was covered with black pepper and or cottonwood bark and a small fire designed to produce the most smoke was made in the hole under the screen. The idea was to produce smoke and not much heat. The meat was then dehydrated without the chance for flies to lay eggs on it.

Once there was enough meat dried in this manner they took one of the stomachs out of the water and began to put the pieces of dried meat into it. The inside of this "stomach bag" was the clean outer side of the organ when the animal had been alive, and as such would not contaminate the meat. Once the "Bag" was filled, the air was squeezed out and the end held while twirled to close the opening and then tied in a knot. This "Bag" was then tied to a tree limb to "shrink wrap" as it dried. These bags were then tied to the horses usually several to a side. The bag kept the dirt and flies out during the week or so ride back home. Once home the bags were tied to the rafters of the house or barn where the mice couldn't get to them and they would stay dry. They would remain good for months in this manner.

To make the meat suitable for consumption it would be taken out and boiled in water with the salt and pepper, cottonwood ash and bark rinsed off. Once the salt had been leached out, the meat could then be cut up and used in stews.

Using this process Maidu hunters could take several elk down and render the meat into light enough loads to be carried back to their villages for winter consumption.

Manzanita berries could be eaten raw or dried and made into a flour used to make a sort of bread.

The Maidu also ate manzanita berries off the bush or crushed them into a flour that could be used to make a sort of flat bread.

Soap Weed

The soap weed could be peeled like an onion and then cut up and placed in a basket which would be placed in a stream to leach out the acid. Once done the cuttings were usually cooked for consumption. A side benefit of in the leaching process was that depending on the water flow and size of stream, the soap weed chemicals would drug the fish making them easy to pick up.

Wild Potato

The native potato called So Kop Mi grows in meadowlands higher in elevations (4,000 feet and a bit higher). The tubers are about the size of a peanut are high in starch; they were typically washed, boiled and made into a paste or later cooked in a frying pan. This species was encouraged by the Maidu by weeding and transplanting.

Buckeye Nuts

This small tree produces large nuts that are crushed and leached before being cooked and eaten. It is a matter of note that the Buckeye trees were new to No Po Chitta Toma (Columbia Flat) at the time of the Gold Rush.

While the species is native to California it had only recently arrived in this area and the local Maidu had to ask tribes from the South how to process it for consumption. It is now numerous and common in areas over one hundred miles to the North of No Po Chitta Toma today.

It would be interesting to know why it migrated but we only know that it did because of the references to it by the Native Californians.

Black Oak, White Oak, Chink-o-pin

and several species of Live Oak produce edible acorns, The factors affecting the edibility of acorn's are the levels of tannic acid that must be leached out in order to make it edible (this acid level varies by species) and the size and accessibility of the acorns; plus of course personal preferences as some stands and species "Tasted" better than others.

The process of leaching the acid and cooking the material into an edible mush may seem time consuming to us, but the durability of this foodstuff in storage with a shelf life of three to four years and its availability made it a staple.

"Digger Pine," recently renamed to Grey Pine, was one of the primary sources of Pine Nuts for tribes living West of the crest of the Sierra Nevada and all the way to the coast.

The nuts from Sugar Pine were collected by gathering them after they fell. Due to the extreme height of Sugar Pine and Ponderosa Pine the gathering of the cones was impractical, so only a short opportunity existed once the (seeds) pine nuts were falling to gather these species.

On the East side of the Sierra Nevada the primary pine nut producing species was the Pinyon Pine.The Pinyon Pine is a short tree and the cones could be gathered before they opened up and cast their seed, made for a longer process.

A Buckeye nut and the leaves.

and more efficient gathering

Various species of Fire Pine, including Pinus Attenuata, were used as well; these are typically short trees with large cones but the extraction of their nuts was more complicated. This species typically only open up their cones scales after a wildfire. This process typically required roasting the cones in a fire then setting them on a cleared stone surface where the scales would open and drop their seeds, then they could be collected.

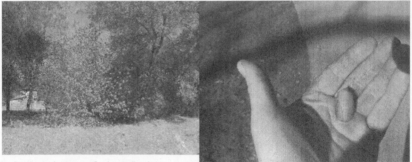

The Buckeye is more of a large bush or small tree and produces a large crop of nuts usually falling before December.

A White Oak acorn shown here is smaller than that of the Black Oak but larger than most species of Live oak.

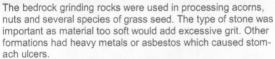

"Digger Pine Cone" filled with pitch and having sharp scales..

The bedrock grinding rocks were used in processing acorns, nuts and several species of grass seed. The type of stone was important as material too soft would add excessive grit. Other formations had heavy metals or asbestos which caused stomach ulcers.

Pictured above a Grey Pine cone that squirrels have "Shucked" to remove the pine nuts located under the scales.

Pictured below is a pile of scales left by squirrels opening up and "Shucking" the cones. This was typical for people in processing this food as well and caused the reference "Digger Indians". The people could obtain a high protein food in fairly large quantities by this process. It was also common to locate the squirrel's cash of nuts and there by use the Squirrel's labor for the nut extraction.

A Maidu story as told around my Grandfather's Sawmill in Spanish Flat in the 1930's . "Don't trust the Rattlesnake he has a forked Tongue"

This timeless story as told around the Saw Mill in the 1930's.

In the early times, animals and people could talk to each other same as us now. They had their problems the same as we do today.

One day Rattlesnake (Sola) was out sunning himself on a rock when Coyote (Dappe) came over and sat down by Rattlesnake. Down the hill from them they watched Hawk (Buklak) fly down and grab a jackrabbit. Coyote said to Rattlesnake "I sure like Jackrabbit meat, Hawk can fly and it annoys me because he is so good at getting Jackrabbits."

Rattlesnake decided to go down to a squirrel hole. He was slithering up beside the hole when Hawk (Buklak) stopped down beside him with a Jack Rabbit he had just killed and began to eat.

Rattlesnake watched Hawk eat when off in the distance they saw Coyote running down a ground squirrel. Hawk said, "I like ground squirrel but I can't dig or run fast like Coyote. Coyote is always boasting about how fast he can run and all the squirrels he has caught."

Rattlesnake thought about it awhile, then he asked Hawk if he could have some of the jack rabbit meat. Hawk wanted to be a nice neighbor so he gave a piece to Rattlesnake. Rattlesnake took the piece with him and went over to Coyote. Coyote was tired out from running and had only one ground squirrel to show for it.

Rattlesnake said to Coyote "You know, some day you might not be fast enough to get a squirrel and then you would go hungry. With Hawk flying all around you know the number of jackrabbits will get fewer and fewer till none are left".

"Yeh, you're right Rattlesnake, it is hard to get ground squirrels" said Coyote. Rattlesnake said "I can get you jackrabbit meat, you interested?" Coyote said "Yes, I'm interested."

"Here you can have some of mine" said Rattlesnake. While Coyote was eating the jackrabbit meat Rattlesnake asked if he could have the ground squirrel Coyote had. Coyote wanted to be a good neighbor and said he could have it.

Rattlesnake then took the ground squirrel to Hawk. Rattlesnake said to Hawk "I have a ground squirrel for you." Hawk was delighted and began eating the ground squirrel. Rattlesnake then told hawk that he had another gift for him. It was a jacket made from soap weed fibers to keep him warm. Hawk didn't want to be rude so he agreed to let Rattlesnake put the jacket on him. Then Rattlesnake asked if he could have the rest of Hawks jack rabbit meat. Hawk didn't want to be rude and said that was OK.

Rattlesnake took the jackrabbit meat back to Coyote. Rattlesnake said to coyote, "I have some more jackrabbit meat for you." Coyote thanked Rattlesnake and began to eat the meat. Rattlesnake asked Coyote "Will you do something for me?" Coyote asked "What do you want?" Rattlesnake asked if he could put a harness on Coyote to attach a rope to so that Coyote could help turn a rock over for Rattlesnake to get at the squirrel nest under it. Coyote thought this was fair enough and let Rattlesnake put the harness on him and tie the rope to the rock. Soon, they had the rock turned enough that Rattlesnake could go into the squirrels nest. Soon Rattlesnake came back up with several small lumps in him (baby squirrels) and an adult squirrel that had tried to protect its nest.

Rattlesnake said "This worked so well. Can I keep this rope on you to do this again in awhile?" Coyote marveled at the number of squirrels and said it was OK. Rattlesnake then tied the loose end of the rope around Coyote's leg. Then Rattlesnake took the adult ground squirrel with him to Hawk.

Hawk saw Rattlesnake coming and said "This is a nice jacket but I can't fly with it." Rattlesnake said "You wont need to fly, I will take care of you, here is another ground squirrel."

Hawk thanked Rattlesnake and then said "But I like to fly." Rattlesnake said to Hawk "You see Coyote down there, he can't run any more so there will be plenty of squirrels." Hawk could see Coyote hobbling around and he had to agree that Coyote wouldn't be getting many squirrels now.

Rattlesnake then went down to Coyote. Coyote saw Rattlesnake coming and said " Hey, Rattlesnake I can't run with this rope tied on my leg." Rattlesnake said to Coyote "You see hawk up there, he can't fly any more so he won't be getting so many jackrabbits now." Coyote looked at Hawk and agreed. Rattlesnake then told Coyote to trust him and he would take care of him.

Then Rattlesnake went down to talk to the ground squirrels and Jackrabbits. Rattlesnake told the little animals that he would release Hawk and Coyote

unless they paid tribute to him. Rattlesnake told the little animals that he wanted a few of their babies because he couldn't eat the adults but that when one of the adults died of old age or disease he needed them to give him the bodies to take to Hawk and Coyote.

The little animals didn't like the idea of giving some of their babies to Rattlesnake, but it did mean that they wouldn't have to work as hard and live in danger of being hunted by Hawk or Coyote, so they agreed.

Time went on and Rattlesnake grew bigger and bigger. The bigger he got the more menacing he looked and the more little baby jack rabbits and ground squirrels he demanded. With fewer babies living to be adults soon there were squirrels and jack rabbits.

One day Coyote and Hawk were together when Fat Rattlesnake lumbered past them. They asked Rattlesnake why they were getting fewer and fewer squirrels and jackrabbits to eat. Rattlesnake said "Don't blame me there are fewer jack rabbits and ground squirrels these days." Hawk and Coyote could see he was right but they were hungry, lean and there was nothing they could do but beg Rattlesnake for more food.

One day a man (Majdykym) came into the valley. Man was special because the Creator (Gak-ini) made him with the ability to think like Gak-ini. Man saw Hawk and Coyote and sat down beside them. Man asked why Hawk was wearing a jacket and wasn't flying and why Coyote was all tied up.

They told him that Rattlesnake was running things and that he was taking care of them so they didn't need to fly or run. Man sat there awhile looking around. Then he asked Hawk and Coyote why there were so few jackrabbits and ground squirrels around? Hawk and Coyote said they didn't know but that the number of these animals had started to decline after Rattlesnake began to run things.

Man went over to a Ground Squirrel and asked him what was happening? ground squirrel explained what Rattlesnake was doing and how now they had to give him almost all of their babies these days and he was still wanting more. Man then told ground squirrel to tell the jackrabbits and other squirrels to come up to the rock where Hawk and Coyote were.

When all the animals had arrived man stood up and explained that the great Gak-ini had set things up so that Coyote could run and Hawk could fly and that the little animals wouldn't have to give all their babies to Rattlesnake. Man warned the animals that Rattlesnake spoke with a double tongue (reference to the forked tip of the snakes tongue).

Man said "The words of Rattlesnake mean something different than they sound like. You should do what you are good at and not depend on handouts from Rattlesnake. He is the only one who profits from this situation, this is not the way Gak-ini intended. Man then set Hawk and Coyote free to make their living by themselves.

So now Rattlesnake has to hide under a rock when he sees a Hawk or Coyote. When Rattlesnake gets near a ground Squirrel nest the Squirrels come out yelling and throw sticks and dirt on him.

To be free allows you to fly, run and do what you do best, it is taking a chance but it is the way the great Gak-ini intended. Once you give up your freedom for the security promised by the double tongue you have less and are in the end more insecure.

The Maidu Creation Story

The world of the Maidu from Po-No-Chitta Toma towards Syhylim Toma over Hekeke Sarwe, Pano's hangi. The Mountain (Yamanim) up stream (natomas) of Columbia Flat and Mosquito over looking bear's house.

In the early days of the world all the people and animals were able to talk to one another. This didn't do them any good, though as they were all fighting each other. The Creator (The Great Gak-ini) decided that they needed some rules and order on earth.

Pano (Bear)

Joskopim
(Grey Fox)

The Gak-ini came out of the reflection (Hinch-esimin) of Lake Almanor (Momdanim) at the (Yspolpolpolim) magical boiling water. He called on the wild goose (Lok-noma) to go out and tell everyone to come to the (Hangi) big house in Moon Flat (Po-no-chitta-Toma) village (Kochacruchu) of the people (Majdykym) man for a meeting.

When everybody was present the Creator asked how they were doing (Minki Kodojdi Hesasakade)?

A woman (Kylem) of the people said we are having a little (tibim) trouble (Yswalulum), nobody has any rules to follow and we are getting nowhere.

Five others including Molloko the vulture and Joskopim the Grey Fox said this was true.

The creator (Gak-ini) began to lay out the rules for everybody to follow and everybody began to agree when Joskopim (Grey Fox) noticed that Bear (Pano) and Rattlesnake (Csa-can-tay Yswal) were not there.

The Creator (Gak-ini) was irritated and sent Molloko (Vulture) up into the sky to look for them.

Molloko saw Pano running across the Valley (Kojo) toward the mountain (Yamanim). The Creator (Gak-ini) with Syym (Coyote) tracking to the Mountain (Yamanim) and hollered for Pano to come out. Porcupine (Ch onim ya-manim) said he could hear the rattle (Csa-can -tay) of Rattlesnake (Csa-can-tay Yswal) over there under a rock. Gak-ini moved the rock and saw Rattlesnake (Csa-can-tay Yswal) and put his foot on his head.

Wilki or Tannu (Deer)

Just then Valley Quail (Hekeke) began to flutter and squawk as Pano (Bear) jumped out of the bush (Pam) and tried to run away, Gak-ini reached out and grabbed Pano's tail. Pano was struggling so much that finally Pano's tail came off with blood (kichau) spraying on Gak-ini's hand. Gak-ini lost his footing as Pano's tail came off and Rattlesnake (Csa-can-tay Yswal) slithered out and went under a big boulder.

This is why Pano has such a short tail and why Rattlesnake (Csa-can-tay Yswal) has a flat head and are the two creatures in the woods who will bite you. As Man (Majdykym) is a reflection (Hinch esimin) of Gak-ini (The Creator) the skin on his hands and arms, if we works outside, gets sort of red colored because of Pano's blood (kichau).

Pano (Bear) sleeps in the forest but enjoys eating (Sumpiti) Berries (Coffee berry). In the picture to the left the closest ridge is covered in (Sumpiti Pam) Coffee berry Brush.

The Beginning of the World

A translation of the Maidu story.

In the beginning there was nothing but water (Momim). No sun, stars or moon (Pompokom).

One day something came floating up and it was turtle. Down from the sky on a rope of feathers, came a being that shined like the sun, this was the Creator Gak' ini. When he stepped onto turtle's back, Gak ini's face was covered so that turtle (K-ocos) could not see it. Gak ini sat down and was quiet for a long time until turtle asked "Where do you came from?" Gak ini said "I come from the sky above."

Turtle (K-ocos) thought about it a bit. Then he asked Gak ini "Can you make some dry land for me so I could get out of the water?" Gak ini thought about it and said he would. Gak ini said as to how he didn't know but if turtle wanted some dry land, Gak ini needed some dirt to make it with. Turtle said that if Gak ini would tie a stone to his left arm he would dive down and get some. Gak ini tied a rope to turtle who thought and said, "If the rope is to short I will jerk it once for more length but when I have a full load of dirt I will jerk it twice for you to haul it up."

Albino's like this deer with pink eyes and clear hooves were considered religious by all Native American tribes. For the Maidu and other tribes the hide of an albino deer was part of the marriage ceremony as it was like the animals described in this story who were newly created.

Turtle went down into the water and after six years he came back up covered with green slime but all the dirt had washed off his back and the only dirt was under his claws. Gak ini took this little dirt and rolled it in his hand into small balls. These he placed on the stern of a small raft. Gak ini left and returned three times, so the small balls grew. The third time he came back, the ground was rather large. On the fourth time it was as big as the world, with mountains all around it.

Turtle was up on the ground and asked if he could have some light to see with. Gak ini said to turtle to look to the East and he Gak ini would ask his sister to come up. Soon it grew light and K-ocos asked which way Gak ini's sister would go. Gak ini thought about it and said," I'll ask her to get up high then go down over there in the West".

After Gak ini's sister had gone up high and then went down out of sight in the West it grew dark again. K-ocos asked if Gak ini could do anything more? Gak ini said he would ask his brother Moon (Pombokom) to come up in the East then go high and go back down just as his sister had done.

Gak ini asked turtle how he liked all this? Turtlewas pleased but asked Gak ini if this was all that he could do?

Gakini said there was a lot more he could do and he called out the stars by name, then he made one tree with twelve kinds of acorns on it. This tree grew at Duram and K-ocos and Gak ini sat under it for two (peen) days.

Then they walked off to see the rest of the world. Gak ini made birds and more trees as well as the animals. After this, Gak ini said "I am going to make

people". Gak ini took some red earth and mixed it with water and made two (peen) figures out of it. One figure was a man (Majdykym) and the other woman (Kylem). Gak ini laid down and set the man on his right side and the woman on his left. The next morning woman began to tickle him so he got up and put a piece of wood in the ground which burst into fire.

The two people were very white with pink eyes and black hair, their teeth shone bright and they were very handsome. Gak ini named the man Kuksu and the woman Morning Star Woman (Banak'am Mo-lo Kyle).

When Coyote (Syym) first saw the people he asked Gak ini how he made them? Gak ini told Syym how he had done it and syym thought to himself that isn't difficult I'll do it myself. Syym did it and the next morning the woman poked Syym in the ribs but Coyote (Syym) laughed. Gak ini showed up and saw the glass eyed people and told Syym that he should not have laughed. Syym told Gak ini he hadn't laughed and so he told the first lie in the world.

After awhile there were a lot of people made and Gak ini wanted things to be easy for them. At this time Gak ini didn't come to the world as often as he had in the beginning and he usually only came at night to talk to Kuksu. One night Gak ini told Kuksu to take all the people to a lake near there but that Kuksu would be a very old man by the time he reached the lake.

The next morning Kuksu led all the people to the lake and just as Gak ini had said Kuksu turned very old and he fell into the lake and sank out of sight. Then the ground shook and the waves grew large when suddenly Kuksu appeared out of the lake and he was young again!

Gak ini appeared and told the people that if they did as he told them they could come to this lake when they grew old and it would make them young again.

For a long time things were easy and all the women had to do was put their baskets out at night and in the morning they would be full of nice warm food ready to eat.

Then one day Coyote (Syym) came by and said, "This isn't good I have a better way."

Syym explained that the people needed to burn their property for the dead, so that the widows can be free.

Syym took all the peoples' baskets and hung them on poles and made

everything ready. He then told the people that they must play games and to start the games with a foot race. Only Kuksu did not attend for he sat in his house very sad, as he knew that death was going to come to the world.

Rattlesnake (Sola) came to Kuksu and asked him what to do, as everything was spoilt. Kuksu didn't answer. Rattlesnake said he would do what he thought was best. Sola (Rattlesnake) went out where the race was to be run and when Coyote's son came running by, Rattlesnake raised up his head from a hole and bit the boy on the ankle. The boy died in a minute.

The spectators saw Coyote's son fall and said that he must be so ashamed that he does not dare get up. Coyote (Syym) went over to his son and saw that he was dead, and this was the first death in the world.

The people did not understand and brought the boy over to syym who began to cry. They did the same, these were the first tears in the world.

Coyote took his son to the lake and threw him in but the body only floated in the water (momim). Then Syym took his son to Kuksu and asked him to bring him back to life. Syym gave Kuksu four (cyyj) bags of beads and several bear skins.

Syym begged Kuksu for five (maawyk) days before Kuksu came out of his house.

Kuksu gave all the bags of beads back to Syym and then wrapped the boy in a skin and tied it shut. Then he dug a grave and put the body in it and covered it up. Kuksu told everyone that this was what they would have to do until the world was remade.

Some time after this the people suddenly began to speak different languages. Every couple spoke the same language but they could not understand the language of other couples. Gak ini had come to Kuksu the night before and told him what to do. Kuksu came out in the morning and he could speak all the languages. Kuksu then called all the people together and told them how to hunt and cook. Gave them their laws and set the time for the festivals and dances. Then Kuksu sent the warriors to the North; the singers to the West, the flute players to the East, the dancers to the South. Kuksu told them that was where they were to live.

These people, who spoke different languages and were sent to the different parts of the world by Kuksu, were the ancestors of the different tribes.

Language and Names used by the Native Peoples of El Dorado and Amador Counties.

In doing research on the Maidu, Miwok and Washoe people who lived in El Dorado County I found some interesting things as related to place names and language.

I have tried my best to put the correct names to places and people but in doing so I found several interesting anomalies.

The area of Sly Park to El Dorado located in El Dorado County was the intersection of three Tribes. The Washoe from the East, the Maidu from the North and the Miwok from the South.

As such most places in this area have at least two names as in a Miwok and a Maidu name. Some places have a mixture of the two languages. In my area No-Po Chitta-Toma is Moon Flat which in checking the research available checks out as Maidu (Nisenan) yet nearby Hekeke Toma is a mixture as Hekeke is the Miwok word for Valley Quail and Toma is Maidu.

In many stories from both the Maidu and Miwok some animal names from the other language are used frequently. The research itself shows that there were many animals that had two or more names that sound nothing like the other, even in the same language. For example deer in Maidu can be dypp'e or k'ut' and bear can be Pano or kappa. One possible reason for this two name listing might have been an identification of Grizzly Bear from Black Bear but in the research I have found Pano was the Grizzly. (But that doesn't hold true either.)

The Last Chief of the Maidu, Coppa Hembo said to be a translation of "Bear Killer" may give us a clue. Coppa is obviously a derivative of Kappa and is Maidu for bear however the story was that he killed a "Grizzly Bear" in Mosquito Creek below Swansborough so this may not be true. Also the last part of his name (Hembo) doesn't sound anything like Killer, or anything similar in Maidu. Since the story was that Coppa Hembo was the son of a refugee Washoe woman it would be logical to explain this as a derivative of the Washoe language.

A similar situation would be the border area of Italy, Bavaria, France and Switzerland. The names for places and people would be confusing to interpret using a German dictionary from Berlin and an Italian dictionary from Naples. Both the regional accents and mixing of these with French influences can make it difficult.

Another factor to consider is that the primary source of the information local to Pleasant Valley was from Mary Hunter. Mary was a full-blood Northern Miwok who lived near the Pleasant Valley School house. She was fluent in the Northern Sierran Dialect of Miwok and the Southern Nisenan dialect of Maidu but at the time she was interviewed by Hugh Littlejohn, she was too decrepit to move very much and her speech was unclear.

We owe a great deal to the efforts made by the early researchers and historians but they had an impossibly difficult task.

In the stories I used the names were at times inconsistent for some species. For example, the coyote was referred to as Syym in several stories and as dappe in others. In reference material, Syym was listed as the term for dog. It is my extrapolation that the original speaker may not have used the term dappe for coyote, as it may have been a Northern Maidu term, or the speaker didn't know the different term existed for dog and coyote in their language.

Another problem animal is the Rattlesnake. In some stories and text it is listed as Sola while in one story it was Csa-can-tay Yswal. As far as I was able to determine, Csa-can-tay is the word for rattle and Yswal is the generic term for snake. It would be my guess that this was a name used later, and was influenced by the American reference for the animal while Sola was the earlier identification or a Northern Concow Maidu dialect term.

It was my intent to be as accurate as I could possibly be. So I have used the word or term used in the story that was provided me. That these terms are not completely consistent

from one story to another was something I decided
not reconcile for the previous reasons.

It is my hope that those readers who have an interest in these languages, to please contact the ongo-
ing language research or at least purchase the com-
pilations of language texts available, which I have
listed in the reference section of this book.

A little about the Author Guy Nixon (Redcorn).

Guy Nixon was born and raised in El Dorado County California. After serving in the US Navy he graduated from Sacramento State with a Bachelor degree in Biology with an emphasis in Wildlife Management and a minor in Geology. He worked for the US Forest Service for 14 years starting with timber and later conducting the first comprehensive Abandoned Mine Survey for the El Dorado National Forest. Later he led the first extensive trail survey of the Georgetown Ranger District of the El Dorado National Forest. This was followed with work at the Institute of Forest Genetics for three years as well as serving as a Forest Protection Officer. He later worked as a substitute teacher and for the Special Education Department. All this while working with his father (Bill Nixon) operate his Grandfather's sawmill.

Guy has always had a great interest in history, wildlife and geology, using the technology of the stone age to actually hunt and process deer with these tools.

Living in the home of his Grandfather Guy has always been fascinated with the history of the local Maidu, who live around there and whose old stories were remembered by his Grandfather and father from back in the 1930's

Pictured above is the Author's Grandfather's Grandfather, Bill Nixon, with the Second Osage delegation to Kansas. To the left Guy with his youngest son and a bear they took near the older sons school bus stop that was being aggressive.

I would like to thank my family for much of this information. My father, Bill Nixon, took me along on his many field trips with his work on water systems all over the Western part of North America. He would stop to show me the history and talk to the locals who knew it. My Grandfather, Bill Nixon, grew up in Oklahoma on the Osage reservation and was a graduate of Haskell Indian College. His perspective has influenced my Father and I in researching history. His namesake my Grandfathers, grandfather Bill Nixon served the Osage Tribe in it's armed forces, police and later as a Supreme Court Judge. The history from the Native American point of view doesn't start when the wagon train or ship arrived and therefore has a more complex set of forces in place. Once a person has the whole story the many parts of the story make sense.

Spring 1940

My sons from right to left, Scott, Bryan, Jacob, myself and the neighbor Joseph Barnhart with Skipper a stock killing bear from our area.

BIBLIOGRAPHY

ORAL SOURCES

Adams, Rick Nisinan Shaman

Allred, Pauline Osage Museum

Bergen, Frank Ely Nevada Historian

January, Betty Clarksville Historian

Lewis, Charley Local Historian

Nixon, Bill my Grandfather

Poor, Bill Store owner at Louisville

Paiute members of the Nixon Indian Reservation, who were alumni friends of my father at the University of Nevada Reno.

Redcorn, Katheren Osage Museum

Sailor, John

Sanders, David Historian

Schuster, Myrtle a Miwok friend of my Mother who attended the same church in El Dorado as we did.

Timm, Bill owner of the Alhambra Gold Mine Spanish Flat California.

Wheldon, George local Geologist

Wooden Boat Foundation, 431 Water St. Port Townsend, WA 98368

Plus many more people I can't remember the names of.

BOOKS AND PUBLICATIONS

Bailey, L.R. Indian Slave Trade in the Southwest, Western Lore Press Los Angeles California 1966

Baird, David W. A Creek Warrior for the Confederacy the Autobiography of Chief George G.W. Grayson, University of Oklahoma Press, Norman, Oklahoma 1988

Breweer, William H. Up and Down California In 1860-1864, University of California Press, Los Angeles 2003

Brooks, James F. Captives and Cousins Slavery, Kinship, and Community in the Southwest Borderlands, Published for the Omohundro Institute of Early American History and Culture. 1996

Burrows, Jack. Black Sun of the Miwok, University of New Mexico

196

Press 2000

Carroll, Ronald. Principals of Conservation Biology, Sinauer Associates, INC, Sunderland, Massachusetts 1994

Carter, Forrest. Watch for Me on The Mountain, Bantam Doubleday Dell Publishing Group, Inc, New York, New York 1978 Cherokee Carter Corporation

Cottrell, Steve. Civil War in the Indian Territory, Pelican Publishing Company, Gretna, Louisiana 1995

Cunningham, Frank. General Stand Watie's Confederate Indians, Naylor Company San Antonio, Texas 1959

Eatough, Andrew. Central Hill Nisenan Texts with Grammatical Sketch, University of California Press, Berkeley, California 1999

Final Report to Congress No.37, Sierra Nevada Ecosystem Project, University of California Davis.1996

French in the Southwest 1540-1795 (Colledge Studies) Texas A and M University Press 1955

Gernes, Phyllis. Hidden in the Chaparral, Published by Phillis Gernes 1979

Goodwyn, Lawrence. The South Central States, Time-Life Publishing Company New York New York 1967

Mayer, John J and Brisbin, Lehr. Wild Pigs of the United States, University of Georgia Press, Athens, Georgia 1991

McChesney, Mike, The Jesuits, The Treasure Hunters Reference 2011

Mathews, John Joseph. The Osages, University of Oklahoma Press Norman, Oklahoma 1961 Wah'Kon Tah Norman, Oklahoma 1932

Moorhead, Max. Spanish Deportation of Hostile Apache, Arizona and the West, Vol 17 p205-220 Published by the Journal of the Southwest 1975

Peabody, George An Anthology of Historical   Stories. The El Dorado County Print Shop, Placerville,   CA 2008

Pearson, Ruth Farrell Higgens. Oak Run and Over The Hill. Millville Historical Society, Millville, California 2006

Ogle, Beverly Whisper of the Maidu. 1998

Reff, Daniel T. Disease Depopulation and Culture Change in Northwestern New Spain 1518-1764, University of Utah Press Salt Lake City Utah 1991

Roosevelt, Theodore. The Rough Riders, Scribner New York New York 1902

Shirley, Glenn. Wiley Green Haines Lawman of the Osage Nation,

Westerner, Behn-Miller Publishers Encino, California 1970

Shakely, Jack. The Confederate War Bonnet, IUniverse, Lincoln, Nebraska 2008

Spencer, John D. The American Civil War in the Indian Territory, Osprey Publishing Company, Oxford, UK 2006

Taylor, Colin F. The Native Americans, Salamander London, UK 1989

Ugarte, Jacob. The Apache Frontier and Spanish Indian Relationsin Northern New Spain 1764-1791, Waman OK, University of Oklahoma Press 1969

Warren, Steven L. Last Raid at Cabin Creek, Fusion Media Productions, Spokane, Washington 1992

Waugh, John C. Sam Bell Maxey and the Confederate Indians, McWhiney Foundation Press McMurry University Abiline, Texas 1985

Wise, Donald A. 1st Osage Battalion, C.S.A. Oklahoma Historical Society Press, Norman, Oklahoma 1928

World at War Mexican Identities, Insurgents and the French Occupation 1862-1867 By Mark Mureno

MUSEUMS AND LIBRARIES

Bruno's, Gerlach, Nevada (Black Rock Desert)

California State Indian Museum, Sacramento, California Sacramento County

Chawse, California State Park, Amador County

Cherokee National Museum, Telequah, Oklahoma

Duck Water Indian Reservation, Duck Water, Nevada.

El Dorado County Historical Museum, Placerville California

Lava Beds, National Monument, Modoc County, California

Mormon Genealogical Library, Placerville, California

Museum of the Five Civilized Tribes, Okmulgee, Oklahoma

Nevada State Historical Museum, Carson City, Nevada.

Phillips Family Saw Mill, Buzzard Roost Road/Bullskin Ridge, Oak Run California, Shasta County

Placer County Historical Museum, Auburn California

Sutter's Fort, California State Park, Sacramento California, Sacramento County.

University of California, Sacramento State Library, Sacramento, California.
Here I looked up every book, article and paper they had, or could get, on the subject of the Osage Indians for over four years of research. I can't remember the incredible volume of material I looked at.

Special Resources

The Cherokee Heritage Center
21192 S. Keeler Drive
P.O. Box 515
Tahlequah, OK 74465
Phone (918) 456-6007
Fax (918) 456-6165
www.CherokeeHeritage.org

Museum of the Cherokee Indian
589 Tsali Blvd
P.O. Box 1599
Cherokee, NC 28719
Phone (8280 497-3481
Fax (828) 497-4985
Www.cherokeemuseum.org

Pictured above Bill Nixon below his great grandson Bill Nixon.

Osage News
P.O. Box 779
Pawhuska, OK 74056
OsageNews.osagenews.org

National Archives Washington D.C.
700 Pennsylvania Ave. NW
Washington, DC 20408
Phone (1 866) 272-6272

Oswego Historical Society
410 Commercial
Oswego, Kansas 67356
Phone (620) 795-4843

The Cherokee Phoenix
P.O. Bob 948

199

Tahlequah,OK 74465
(918) 453-5269
1-800-256-0671
FAX (918) 458-6136
Www.cherokeephoenix.org

Bishink
The official publication of the Choctaw Nation of Oklahoma
P.O. Box 1210
Durant, OK 74702
(580) 924-8280
(800) 522-6170
FAX (580) 924-4148
Www.choctawnation.com
E-mail; bishinik@choctawnation.com

A sioux bride in her wedding dress

The Canyon Barranca del Cobre in Sonora Mexico

Other books by Guy Nixon (Redcorn)

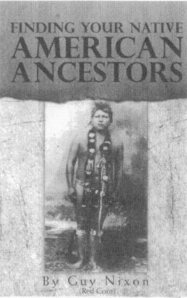

The Wild History of Hell Hole and the Rubicon Country
1848 to 1948
El Dorado and Placer Counties California

Other books by Guy Nixon

Avaliable at

redcorn4440@gmail.com

Heirloom Tales Past and Present, Including Skipper the Stock Killer of Spanish Flat

Saw Milling and Wood cutting for Little Operators

The history of the West from the Natives perspective and the world wide forces affecting them are rarely found in our history books. For the tribes in the West the history before the 1840's is poorly understood and when taken out of context seems to make no sense to the casual reader. In particular the history of the Natives in Northern California seems to be completely overlooked. These people had a turbulent history prior to the Gold Rush of 1849 and while run over in the flood of immigration their history continued . This fascinating part of our Nation's history and the context in which it occurred is the heart of this work.

Made in the USA
Lexington, KY
19 December 2013